RAYFUL EDMOND

Washingon D.C.'s
Most Notorious Drug Lord

Gorilla Convict Publications © 2013
First Printing June 2013

ISBN   978-0-9800687-7-1
        0-9800687-7-0
E-Book: 978-0-9889760-0-9

Cover by Christian Cipollini
Layout by Matt Pramschufer
Printed in the United States of America

Published byGorilla Convict Publications
1019 Willott Road
St. Peters, MO 63376
www.gorillaconvict.com

"Seth 'Soul Man' Ferranti is the truth! Please believe it! He gives it to you raw and uncut and takes the readers to the streets to see how O/G's did it. Seth doesn't glorify the streets he lets the men who ran them tell their story honestly and vividly! Each book I've read of Seth's has given me chills!" **Clifford "Spud" Johnson, author of Kalifornia Luv, Gangsta Twist 1 & 2**

"Being incarcerated is what set Seth's work apart from most prison writers. His method is that of a musician/songwriter who has a greater feel for their work by being immersed in every part of the process. I've watched Seth grow from being a reporter behind the wall to the best biographer/author in his field." **Lamont "Fridge" NeeDum, author of Short Side Blues**

"Outside of experiencing prison for yourself, nothing gives us a better inside look at life behind the walls of America's toughest prisons than the writings of Seth Ferranti. The fact that Ferranti writes about his own experiences and interactions with some of the most notorious inmates of our time gives the prison experience a voice that speaks volumes. Highly recommended." **Mark Silverman, author of Rogue Mobster**

"Seth Ferranti, a victim of an overzealous criminal justice system that runs amuck victimizing the victim on an endless pursuit to blame everyone for America's failed drug war except who really deserves the blame... America. This small town young man with a heart of Gold has made every attempt to assist any and every one reach their dream and goals has been unfairly and unjustly sentenced to twenty-five years. Abused, mistreated and tortured by such age old techniques as 'Diesel Therapy' Seth Ferranti has had no choice but to become the 'Gorilla Convict' to deal with such an animalistic environment while all the while keeping a journal, a log that for the first time takes you and I, the readers, into this dark world of despair." **Michael Mickman Gourdine, author of Chili Pimping in Atlantic City: The Memoir of a Small-Time Pimp**

"Seth Ferranti pulls no punches. His Gorilla Convict: The Prison Writings of Seth Ferranti tells the raw, unadulterated story of life in the belly of the beast." Seth has been incarcerated almost 19 years. At no small personal risk, Seth gets the facts straight from some of the most hardened criminals serving time. The book should be required reading for all contemplating a life of crime." **Mobwriter.blogspot.com**

"Ferranti's writing vividly captures the good, bad and often ugly imagery of real underworld history and characters, as only someone with his access could from behind prison walls." **Christian Cipollini, mafialifeblog.com**

"Seth Ferranti's writing vividly, honestly and revealingly portrays life behind prison walls and beyond." **Will Godfrey, Managing Editor of Thefix.com**

"Authors don't get much realer than Seth Ferranti. Having spent the last twenty years in prison he brings his readers the insider stories of gangsters, mobsters, and convicts. No holds barred, Ferranti tells it like it is to give prisoners a voice." **David Amoruso, Gangsters Inc. www.gangstersinc.nl**

"If you're truly curious about life in America's prison system, you absolutely must read the passionate and engrossing writing of Seth Ferranti." **Ben Osborne, Editor-in-Chief, SLAM Magazine**

"Seth Ferranti writes from the ultimate insider perspective...prison. Over the past decade Ferranti has emerged as one of the most revered true crime authors, writing about some of the nation's most notorious gangsters and kingpins with a unique and authentic voice that brings to life a reality most of us will never know This collection of his writings is a must-have for any true crime enthusiast." **Scott M. Deitche, author Rogue Mobster**

Rayful Edmond

To many in his hometown of Washington, D.C., during his 1980s reign as the city's biggest cocaine and crack dealer, Rayful Edmond was public enemy number one. At the height of Dodge City's brutal crack epidemic in 1987, this 22-year-old man was responsible for distributing 60 percent of the cocaine that flooded the city's streets. In the Chocolate City, Rayful was the undisputed king of cocaine. He was street royalty with a certified gangster resume. At his peak Rayful sold 2,000 keys a week, reaped gross profits of $70 million a month and ran an operation with over 150 soldiers to support him. By his early twenties he had established himself as the city's most notorious drug kingpin. In the high profile and glamorous life he led, champagne flowed like water, trips to Las Vegas, New York and Los Angeles were commonplace and $50,000 shopping sprees were the routine. Rayful personified the big city drug lord and his stature epitomized all the accolades that position demanded. To the mainstream media, he encompassed all that was wrong with the city's crack epidemic, but in the streets Rayful was a hero, an inner-city gangster who made it to the top echelons of the drug trade. A Lucky Luciano, Billy the Kid-type figure. But there were consequences to his reign. His volcanic rise coincided with an unprecedented explosion of street violence and drug addiction in the capital city. The era is remembered for murder, mayhem and bloodshed. Historians have blamed the crack storm that seized D.C. on Rayful, but Rayful maintained he was only trying to help his family live a better life and enjoy the finer materialistic trappings of capitalism that were often denied denizens of the ghetto. To the block huggers, four corner hustlers and hood mainstays Rayful was beloved, even worshipped. His appeal crossed boundaries and he was adored by children and adults alike. But to others he was feared, a man who wreaked havoc on his community. Neighborhood people saw the affects of his crack enterprise outside their front doors and it wasn't pretty. A community divided was in essence, a community destroyed. But regardless of what people thought of Rayful, he was an enigma, the president and CEO of what authorities called "the largest network for cocaine street sales in Washington D.C." He was a gangster legend of epic proportions, until he tarnished his legacy by turning snitch.

Part 1

Beginnings

Rayful Edmond III was born November 26, 1964, a child of the nation's capital. His father, Ray Jr. or Big Ray, was a numbers runner and small-time gambler who spent a lot of time in Philadelphia and Atlantic City once the casinos opened. For a time Big Ray held down a job as a driver for the U.S. Department of Health and Human Services, but he quit in the early 1980s "in order to pursue more lucrative employment on the outside," according to his letter of resignation. The lucrative employment just happened to be dealing drugs, and like they say, "the apple doesn't fall far from the tree." Young Rayful, his only son by Constance "Bootsie" Perry, was cut from the same cloth. He was his father's son in many ways. Emulating the moves, mannerisms and swagger of his dad. Still, he grew up a mama's boy under his mother's tutelage. Rayful was a handsome, gregarious kid who rarely got into trouble. He did well enough in school, but he was predestined to get into the life.

Before Rayful was born, members of his family ran

one of the largest numbers operations in D.C. "Rayful comes from a long line of hustlers," Mr. T says. And police concurred, reporting that the Edmond family was linked to old-time drugs and numbers rings, which operated in the 1950s and 1960s. A culture of crime was embedded in Rayful from an early age, and this impacted and influenced his upbringing.

For young Rayful, hustling was in his blood. Once he got started he would go on to be the Don Dada of all Washington D.C. hustlers. The capital's top dope boy, past, present and future. A man whose legacy would live on forever in the annals of gangster lore. But in his youth, he was just a young black kid growing up in the Chocolate City. Trying to survive the ghetto and make a name for himself at the same time. His background wasn't typical for the hood, still it sufficed.

Both his parents worked government jobs, but they moonlighted in the drug trade. His uncles were heavy in the numbers racket and this involvement slowly led them into the illegal drugs market. It was a family affair in the Edmond household and they made no secrets about it. Relatives in the life who were involved in the drug game, rotated in and around him at all times.

Ray was one among many in a big family, growing up with six brothers and sisters. "All of us were loving and caring people," Rayful said. "We were ordinary people just like everyone else in Washington D.C." To Rayful his upbringing might have been ordinary, but he was being groomed from the jump. Some parents want their kids to be lawyers, but for others a drug lord is viewed as a successful occupation at the top of the social ladder. From the start Rayful was soaking up the nuances of the game. With this pedigree, he was destined to become a ghetto star.

Growing up in the Northeast quadrant of D.C., Rayful was bred to be a hustler. Some kids served apprenticeships in carpentry or construction or follow their fathers into the military or police force, but Rayful served his apprenticeship as a student of narcotics, learning the intricacies of the game as a child at his father's knee. Some kids go to school, others like Rayful get schooled in the streets.

"The majority of our crew were born and raised in that area. Growing up in the neighborhood was no different than any other; you know block parties, barbecues. A lot of the older gangsters would look out for us when we were young. They showed us how to conduct ourselves. Their number one rule was always keep your mouth shut! That worked for some, but not for others. One thing I can say about our hood was that it was very close-knit." Antonio "Yo" Jones, who became the top enforcer for Rayful's crew said.

Rayful, like his other homeboys, grew up in the poverty stricken district and learned to hustle to get by. His mom, Bootsie, sold illegal pills that were called "poor peoples crack." Rayful would stand on the corner helping his mother, as she plied her trade. Mother and son were inseparable. As much as Ray learned from his father, it was his mother that imparted the necessary lessons and knowledge of the streets that would help him take his game to the highest levels. She was his muse and confidant in so many ways.

With his parents playing a major role in the early education of the future drug kingpin, Rayful's path was set. Their careful nurturing would reveal a prodigy. To some hustling and the drug game come natural. Rayful took to it very fluidly. Bootsie, the unlikely matriarch of what would become Washington's most prominent crime family, raised Ray to become a hustling icon. He became her pride and joy.

His genius was evident early on. Rayful's childhood was filled with episodes of crime such as the lottery/numbers operations ran by his family, juxtaposed with hardcore ghetto living and surviving by any means to get by. But to him it was routine. He knew nothing else. "He learned the business from his relatives at an early age, counting money and holding drugs." Mr. T says.

Clearly a product of his upbringing and environment, Ray became a street smart, cunning young man from a large, tight-knit family that exposed him to the criminal underworld and all its facets at a young age. He was groomed to be a king of the streets. He was a pampered child who was treated like royalty. "I was spoiled to death," Rayful said. "It was cool because I was the little baby brother. I was king. I had anything I wanted."

In 1975, he attended Hamilton Junior High where he met Royal Brooks and the two established a lifelong friendship. Royal, who Rayful looked up to, said that Edmond would brag that he could package cocaine quickly because "he was raised bagging stuff." Rayful was proud of the skills he learned in his youth and he was ready to put those skills to the test.

By the age of 13, Rayful started getting money. He would pay attention to the old heads from his family and absorb all the game he could listening to their tales of the street life. "He saw the fast money or saw them driving big cars and he said, 'Hey, man, how did you do this? Or how did you get that?'" Bootsie said. The future king had an extensive group of tutors. They provided the lessons and Rayful became a straight A student and valedictorian of the class.

His family was warm and extended, they all gathered at his grandmother's house at 407 M Street Northeast, a neighborhood of brick row houses across from Florida Avenue, where the city's bustling wholesale food market was located. There were summer crab feasts on the stoops and big turkey dinners on Sunday afternoons. It was a Washington, D.C. affair, a bustling and active lifestyle that centered on the neighborhood. His upbringing impacted him. Family and friends were important to Rayful. It defined who he was. That and getting money consumed him.

Edmond recalled the summer nights on M Street with his family when they would go down to Hains Point, have picnics at Lake Fairfax and get crabs from Morgon's Sea Food on the waterfront, with pride. He remembered the mountains of food his family would cook on Thanksgiving, a holiday that fell on or near his November 26th birthday. As he grew up, he developed a taste for good times and the key to good times in his opinion was money. Coming of age in the capitalistic 80s, Reaganomics were paramount in Rayful's mind. He had that "hustle hard" mentality long before studio gangsta's like Rick Ross.

Throughout high school Ray was book smart. Not a nerd, but the popular type. He could have succeeded at anything he wanted, but he chose the drug game. Thinking logically, he listened well and paid close attention to detail. Rayful was one of those children that was born to be sharp. Academics weren't for him though. He loved basketball more than books. He started playing in the Boys Club leagues at 12, and though he never made it past six feet, he could pop the ball in from every corner of the court.

He was a very good basketball player, but the streets pulled at him with their lure of fast money and faster women. It was all he heard about and all that he wanted. Being shown the ropes at an early age he was ready to dive in. "My mom and dad taught me the drug trade." Rayful said. "That's all my life was- school, sports and drugs." At a young age Rayful became the Chocolate City's chosen one. Unlike so many prodigies, he lived up to the hype. Like Lebron, he was the real deal.

He sold PCP and pot on 5th and L, and 6th and L, until graduating in 1982 from Dunbar High School. "Rayful was selling weed, like 82." The D.C. hustler says. "People in his family was getting money, but he was just selling weed. He was cool. He was just starting to ball. He was flipping his money, flipping little shit, getting his money up."

His classmates at Dunbar, once the premier black school in the days before desegregation, voted him *Mr. Dunbar*. He was also voted *Most Popular*, *Mr. Sophmore*, *Mr. Junior* and *Best Dressed*. He became the prince of the city. A dashing young hustler who got all the girls, had money to spend and was the life of the party.

Even as a youngster Rayful exhibited that super charisma and charm he became known for. He was the big man on his high school campus. The center of attention. In his mind, the kid from M Street Northeast was out there doing what he had to do to survive; to keep himself clean, to dress sharp and to pay for his three haircuts a week.

If anything, he had panache and style. He was debonair and flashy. He wanted to be popular with the boys, show the ladies a wad of cash and be a big man for the kids on M Street. He would smile and throw hundred dollar bills around, so the kids could buy a new pair of Air Jordans. Life in the district was rough, and Rayful was like a light of sunshine on an otherwise dreary day.

As he gravitated toward the streets and the family business, two of his best friends- Royal Brooks and John Turner- urged Edmond to stay in school. They wanted him to use his basketball skills to get a scholarship. "You'll miss out on something if you don't go to college," one of his coaches told him. "I'm thinking about it," Edmond said. He attended the University of the District of Colombia for a short stint, but Rayful liked the streets; he liked running around, woman chasing him and people talking about him. He liked spending nights at high stakes craps game. For him, being in the streets made him feel alive. He loved the adrenaline rush he got being in the mix, at the center of the action. Rayful lived for the adventure and rush of being in the life. Being a hustler was appealing to him in so many ways. He was making fast money as a youngster and was never going to sit through four years of anybody's college. As Royal and John Turner stayed in school, the friends went their separate ways, but they all stayed in touch. Rayful made sure of that. Their childhood bonds remained intact. Rayful was always loyal.

After enrolling at U.D.C. Rayful dropped out. He tried to make a living as a cook, but that didn't work out. There was no money in it. Rayful needed a ready cash flow. He needed funds to support his lifestyle. Though his mother and father had income from their government jobs- plus the little money his mother said they made hustling drugs- the Edmond family didn't have any real money. Rayful aimed to get it, so his family could live comfortably.

There were all those people who lived in the Edmond's home, "20 or 30 people" including his grandmother, sisters, half-brothers, half-sisters, cousins and aunts. Someone had to feed them all and usually it was Rayful. "He was getting money grinding," the D.C. hustler says. "But he kept his fronts up real good. He stayed flamboyant." Rayful was eating, but he wanted more. He wasn't the type to settle, he was reaching for the stratosphere. To the streets and his family Rayful was the man, but he was still selling hand to hand.

Rayful recalled the summer nights when everyone was at the M Street house and talking about going down to get some crabs. The family would turn to him and say, "Rayful, you got any money?" And Rayful would answer, "Yeah, I got a little bit of money. We'll go." To hear Rayful tell it, his parents were always looking to him for money. So were his brothers and sisters. So were his friends. He became a provider of sorts, the one who looked out for all the rest. "If I had money, I didn't mind giving it to somebody if I got it." He said. Rayful was generous to a fault. In his mind all he was doing was paying bills, taking care of his family and friends, and keeping up his reputation. To Rayful Edmond, money was the key to everything. It was the means to all ends. He just needed more of it.

Hanover Place in Northwest D.C. was where it all started. All the young hustlers gravitated to the block that was known for hustling. Rayful became a mainstay on the block, grinding and getting money. By age 17, Rayful had seven cars. He was balling. Not the world class, out-of-this-world baller he would become, but he was doing it. Acquiring the trappings of ghetto celebrity and living the lifestyle.

"I would buy and cut cocaine into twenty-five and fifty dollar bags." Rayful said. He was a street hustler down on the block getting his. Rayful was slowly expanding his repertoire, trying to get his grind on and stack his money. It was all he knew and he found he was very good at it. His potential in the drug game was only limited by his ambition.

Some parents provide their children with an education and send them out to the world, others guide them into a trade, but Rayful's father taught him by example. In 1984, he called his eldest son to New York City and gave him a kilogram of cocaine. This was Rayful's inheritance, his birthright so to speak. "It all started with his daddy," Bootsie said. With the profits from the first kilo, Edmond bought two more and an empire was born. As his mother put it, "he started off selling hand to hand." But that wouldn't last long. Rayful would graduate from the corner quickly. With his master's degree in the game, advancement up the hierarchy was a lock. Rayful was a CEO in training.

A brisk spring night in 1985 would be Rayful's last on the street. A lean, athletic young man with a narrow face and a precisely trimmed mustache and beard that circled his mouth, Rayful, in a warmup suit and basketball shoes, had a few dime bags of cocaine in his pocket. Midway down the block, a beat up Pontiac pulled up by the curb. Expecting a sale, Rayful approached and asked how much the man wanted. The door burst open and a police officer in plain clothes jumped out. Rayful turned and ran with the cop on his tail.

The two ran down the street, but Rayful was too fast. He rounded a corner onto Florida Avenue, ducked into a Chinese carryout and ditched the three bags of cocaine in a trash basket before the policeman arrived. Rayful turned and flashed a smile at the undercover; he was hardly out of breath, while the undercover cop was breathing heavy. Daily basketball games kept Rayful in great shape. He looked at the cop and put his hands up.

"Keep your hands out of your pockets," the officer said. He stood Edmond up against the brick wall, spread his legs and patted him down. No drugs, no guns, no knives. He booked him on a minor charge and two hours later Edmond was back out on the street. No harm, no foul. With no drugs in his possession, there was nothing to hold him on.

But the close call taught Rayful an important lesson-let the peons handle the bags of coke on the retail level. Rayful was too smart for hand to hand sales. He was CEO material. At age 18, Rayful retired from street sales and set his sights on becoming a major supplier. That was his goal from the start, he was just paying his dues. Rayful lived according to the gospel of his own survival. He knew what he wanted and what he had to do to get there. His credo was- "You do what you have to do to get by and as long as you don't get caught, you're innocent." These were the words he believed in and lived by. They were his mantra and provided his mindset. Old school and time-honored dope game rules handed down from his mentors.

When the city's vice squad infiltrated Hanover Place in 1985 and took down the reigning drug baron, Cornell Jones, Rayful was already in place. He was prepared and ready. He had organized a crew of friends to work for him. Most were childhood buddies who didn't have jobs, needed cash and liked to stay in the neighborhood. "He

didn't have no problem helping you get some money."
The D.C. hustler says. "He was just real open hearted."
Edmond offered his new crew a simple deal. He would
provide them with a steady supply of cocaine for sale
in various amounts, giving them packages to sell on the
street. They would put no money up front, but Rayful
would take most of the profits. It was an easy way to get
into the business, a crude form of franchising.

"Ray and Johnny started this thing together in
Northeast," Antonio "Yo" Jones said in his book *Quiet
As Kept*. "Rayful was getting mad bank on 5th and L
Street, Northeast. They used to operate down near Hayes
Elementary School, which was on 5th and K Street,
Northeast." With a flourishing business model there were
plenty of job applicants. Rayful even ordered t-shirts as
a marketing tool for his salesmen. They read *Top of the
Line*. Rayful did everything first class and catered to his
workers and clientele.

"Ray, Johnny, Jerry and I put together a little tag
team demo," Yo said. "Jerry and I slang coke on 9th
and U Street, Northwest. Ray and Johnny worked 5th
and L Street, Northeast. They were doing real good in
Northeast, but there was a lot of competition. I was one
of the original members of the Rayful Edmond crew.
I lived and will die by the code of honor. In 1984 we
started getting money together in the Northeast section
of Washington. The town was wide open and everybody
was getting paper and we sure as hell weren't going to be
of out the equation."

Taking down Cornell Jones did nothing to contain the
demand for cocaine. The feds just cut off the head, but
the body was still living. His arrest just opened up an
opportunity for Rayful, who became the new head. Jones

had a lieutenant who escaped prosecution also. His name was Tony Lewis, and he was a good friend of Rayful. He lived a few blocks away across New York Avenue. Tony and Rayful decided to join forces.

"I was brought up around strong, stand up older dudes who always showed morals and principles and death before dishonor by example. Rats and weak dudes were never tolerated on our block of Hanover Street, Northwest D.C." Tony Lewis said. Tony was in the same mold as Rayful- a young, intelligent and classy go-getter with street smarts, style and business sense.

"Ray ran the idea of Tony joining forces together with our crew," Yo said. "Tony had his own crew, up on Bates Street, Northwest, but our crew was a little stronger. Tony Lewis was a class act. A money getting young brother with a lot of class. Slim was about getting paper. He was already caked up from his Hanover Place days. Getting together was a plus for both parties. All Tony talked about was money. I took a liking to him the first time we met." The young hustlers would converge to make history. With everyone playing their position they were about to become the biggest crew D.C. had ever seen.

"Tony could dress his ass off," the D.C. hustler says. "He was more quiet, behind the scenes, a real good dude. A scholar and a gentleman." He complimented Rayful in so many ways, just as Yo did on the enforcement tip. With everything in place Tony and Rayful formed a formidable duo. They were both up-and-coming youngsters, who paid their dues and were ready to take over the mantles of drug lord and kingpin. With Hanover Place crawling with feds, Rayful following advice from Yo, moved the operation to Orleans Place.

"Things started to jump off for the better when we moved our enterprise to the infamous Orleans and Morton Place. Ray and his cousin Johnny initially put together a spot on 5th and L Street, Northeast, around the corner from Orleans. While Jerry and I pushed our pack uptown on 9th and U Street, Northwest. We had hands in all kinds of shit during that time, but we still were a team. Both Jerry and I had open cases in court, but we only knew one way to run the streets…hard as shit! I ended up beating my assault with the intent to kill case, but they stepped Jerry back on a marked money case.

"I eventually closed up shop uptown, mainly because I didn't have my partner watching my back any longer and the way I saw it was four eyes were better than two. I rejoined Ray and Johnny back at our stomping ground on 5th and L Street to discuss some new strategies. One of the things I pointed out to Ray was the wide-open style that was displayed. I told him that I was uncomfortable with the way they were in the open and exposed, so we agreed that I would handle all security matters related to the organization from that point forward. The first thing I did was move the organization to the alleyways of Orleans and Morton Place, Northeast. We decided to use the alleys to prevent the kids from being exposed to the criminal activities that we were involved with. The neighborhood loved and respected us for that move." Yo said.

Part 2

Locking it Down

Orleans Place and Morton Place were short, narrow, parallel one way streets connected by a series of alleys, ten blocks due north of the Supreme Court. Florida Avenue, a major east west thoroughfare, was a short block to the north for easy access and fast getaways. The home turf was well suited for dealing. This was the neighborhood where Rayful grew up. He had envisioned setting up a booming retail market there. Rayful hired kids as lookouts and Orleans Place became known as "the strip." "I was the one who invented the strip, so I was in charge of it." Rayful said. The strip was like a drive-thru store. Lots of traffic going in and out constantly. It was here Rayful would make his fortune. He was in position, a budding 18-year-old entrepreneur who turned his neighborhood into cocaine central. Not a wise move in retrospect, but at the time Rayful was 100 percent behind it. As was his crew.

"We moved the pack on Morton and Orleans Place. The neighbors were a little worried at first about our presence, but they knew us all our lives. Ray was one hell of a young man with words. Ray told them that out of respect we were going to be using the alley ways to hustle in at nights, most of the neighborhood gave us their blessing." Yo said. "Ray told me I had total control over everything. I set up two teams to watch the whole neighborhood and put a few people down on 5th and L Street too. The teams brought customers to the block from all over until they knew where we were 24/7. We put this thing right on the map like old Hanover Place. We were moving coke so fast on the strip it was hard just keeping the whole strip supplied." With a team in place and a good plan Rayful discovered a gold mine. With Orleans and Morton Place all his hustling dreams came true. And with no hierarchy in place he was allowed to enforce his will.

"The capital was a free trade zone for drug dealers," a DEA agent said. Unlike New York and Philadelphia, D.C. had no organized crime bosses controlling the drug business and snuffing out the competition. Anyone could get in the game. It was wide open. Rayful knew this and took advantage of the circumstances available. The first blatant outdoor drug markets opened in 1985, often staffed by drug dealers from New York who came down to take advantage of Washington's free market, liberal bail laws.

"In New York the cops take our money, our dope and beat our ass," a New Yorker who frequented D.C. said. "Down here, cops take you in one night and you're back on the street the next day." With the lax laws and enforcement D.C. was becoming a hustler's paradise, exactly at the precise time Rayful was coming into his own. His timing couldn't have been anymore immaculate. He was the right person with the right idea at the right place and time. He was a drug tycoon waiting to happen.

The drug markets popped up in obvious places- public housing complexes, shabby parts of the city and tough street corners east of the Anacostia River. As the drug dealers became entrenched, the police began to lose control of the neighborhoods. In a role reversal, the drug dealers became more relevant and in control than the cops. Men like Yo, Rayful's number one enforcer became feared and respected gangsters who held sway in the city, and with him regulating things in the hood Rayful's power grew.

"I was considered the number one hammer and all security matters fell on my shoulders. That is until my partner Jerry Millington got out of the penitentiary, then we both shouldered the responsibility. I had to bang my pistol a few times to help bring order to the organization. There's always a lame or two out there that we would have to make an example out of periodically. We would strike by any means; knife, gun, baseball bat, whatever the situation presented. I have always been good at setting my mark and enforcing it. Everyone quickly took notice that we were serious about our money." Yo said.

The coke dealers tended to be young, violent, fearless and greedy. They wanted to come up by any means necessary. They were often a part of the neighborhood, ingrained into its ebbs and flow, where as the cops were strangers and viewed as the enemy by poverty stricken residents of the district. The "no snitching" mindset prevalent in the inner-city was perpetuated and promoted, letting the local gun thugs exploit the rank and file citizens. Selling dope and making money were an ends, not a means, and violence was a hazard of the trade. When cocaine became king, the streets of the district turned much meaner.

Rayful Edmond was among the first of the new breed of drug dealers in Washington's disorganized market. He was the epitome of the cool, casual and calculating drug lord. Back then the strip at Orleans Place was a marvel of free market economics. Supply and demand controlled prices, there were no monopolies and rival dealers competed on equal terms, but Rayful would put an end to all that. Everyone would work for him and him only.

"The block was jumping, money was everywhere and we were getting it all, because our crew didn't allow anyone else to work in our hood. We were very territorial and we got all the bank 24/7," Yo said. "We thought we had a vendor's license the way we were slinging coke. 'Fuck 'em.' That was our motto, the police or whoever, we didn't care. We were on a paper chase and no one was going to stop us. That was our mindset. The strip was open 24/7; we had men working around the clock in shifts. Everyone benefited from our consistency and availability. Our crew was the only people allowed to work on the strip. If you wasn't authorized you would have gotten found somewhere. Orleans and Morton Place was an open air drug market, you could get anything desired. We became one with the neighborhood and made sure everyone stayed safe."

To build his organization, Edmond turned inward to his mother, sisters, half-brothers and cousins. From his grandmother's house at 407 M Street, Edmond directed his staff as they stored coke and cash in apartments and houses. His inner enclave processed the cocaine for street sales, packaging, distributing and allotting it to Edmond's street dealers. His dealers made $500 a night and lieutenants $5000 a week. He paid his runners and lookouts $1000 a week. One of his top sellers, still a teenager, owned numerous cars and was making 20 grand a month.

"The strip was our money making haven," Yo said. "We tried to keep the peace in our neighborhood, that way things would run smooth and the cops would only come around to pick up their payoffs. The neighborhood ran smoothly. Johnny kept things in order on M Street and Red Junior, Blue, Mad Dog, Man, Little Gary and Marcus took care of Orleans and Morton Place. I knew everybody in the neighborhood, so Jerry and I asked a few people about using their rooftops for our surveillance crews. The rooftop thing worked real well, because the police could never see where our lookouts were. We went to Radio Shack and bought walkie-talkies with the ear plugs. The lieutenants would always know what was going on. We put men everywhere with walkie-talkies, the block, foot patrols and even men in the alleyways."

Rayful made room for the smokers and the sellers. He had the outlook of a Fortune 500 company executive. He set up shifts and ran his operation like a corporation. He was so organized, he had a lieutenant on each shift. He sold nine to 19 keys a day, around the clock, by implementing three shifts. The strip ran like a family business when Ray was only 19. Ray never had a drought and everyone was on salary. Ray kept all the business records in his head. He could remember transactions down to the dollar. He was applying all that he had learned and succeeding in his chosen profession.

"Overall we had a close-knit group; every relationship has ups and downs though. It's easier to have a close-knit group with guys who share a similar mindset of don't take no shit from anybody and get money by any means.

We did pretty much everything together such as taking trips, clubbing, and just hanging in general." Yo said.

Nobody had ever monopolized the drug trade in D.C. like Rayful. He was a prodigy and became the Chocolate City's favored son. He was the reigning king and cocaine overlord. "He was a superstar in this town coming out of the 12th grade," Smoke, a dude from the era says. "The empire he made illegitimately, just think what he could of done legitimately." In a way Rayful wasted his talents, he could have been so much more, still his public loved him. Rayful had many adoring fans in the city and still does to this day.

When the strip was running at full capacity, dozens of coke dealers sold little bags to customers who came on foot or slowly cruised through in cars with Virginia or Maryland plates. "Seventy, 80, 90 people would be in line on both sides of the streets," Smoke says. "They'd be making four, five grand in five minutes." On busy nights dealers carried out as many as 30 transactions a minute. A woman who worked for Edmond said she remembered selling $25,000 of cocaine on the strip in two hours.

If a police car ventured onto the strip, lookouts would yell, "Olleray, olleray, olleray," Pig Latin for roller. The narrow alleys between the streets were barricaded, so if the cops gave chase on foot they would encounter an obstacle course of old tires, broken down washing machines, trash cans and trip wires. It was all set up to maximize a dealer's profit and prevent the sellers from getting caught.

"Jerry put together all the little defense mechanisms for the alleyways," Yo said. "He would go to the junkyard twice a week, with a U-Haul truck and buy all kinds of shit, like old refrigerators, stoves, bathtubs, anything big, so we could block the alleys up. That way the police couldn't get their cars in there fast enough to catch our workers. We worked that for about two or more years. Every morning the police would send the trash trucks to clean the alleys up."

It was all a part of Rayful's original blueprint. He had it all schemed out, down to the juveniles lobbing foam footballs, that were hollowed out and stuffed with coke, up and down the block as dealers moved $50 bags. He had envisioned it all before he put it in motion. As a youngster growing up he had seen the potential and he made his vision a reality.

Around this drug supermarket, Edmond organized a highly structured dope peddling system. Edmond and his partner, Tony Lewis, bought cocaine in bulk. The kilo sized bricks were transported to the suburban home of Edmond's sister and brother-in-law, where they were cut down to $25 and $50 bags for street sales. Kathy Sellers, Ray's childhood friend, delivered bags to the strip. Middlemen distributed the carefully counted bags to the runners and dealers who actually sold the coke.

A dealer could sell as many as 500 bags a day and generate 25 grand. Managers collected the days receipts and gave them to Sellers, who took the money back to the Edmond family's home in Prince George's County, Maryland. On one occasion Sellers saw Constance Perry feeding 100 grand in small bills into a counting machine. Money was becoming abundant and plentiful. The strip operation was paying dividends and the only people Rayful trusted with the inside of his operation were family members.

Bootsie knew Rayful was getting paid, but she felt it improper to ask Rayful or any other of her children that were working for him, where they were getting large amounts of money. "There are some things you don't just ask your children," she said. "As long as he took care of me I didn't care what he did." And Rayful made sure his high school pals like Royal Brooks and John Turner, who was playing ball at Georgetown, never wanted for anything.

When Royal went away to college in North Carolina, Ray wanted to stay in touch and keep the friendship alive, so he arranged for Royal to make some money by selling drugs down there. Then when Brooks returned to D.C. Ray paid him big bucks to store money and drugs. Ray only trusted his family and long time friends. He knew the drug game bred larceny in the hearts of men less fortunate than himself, so he kept his circle tight.

"Jerry and I didn't give a fuck about nobody because we kept Rayful safe." Yo said. "That was our job and we were the best at it hands down. Jerry and I never had a problem with getting down and dirty for our crew. Our crew depended on us always being at our best. Ray knew he needed me and I knew I needed him. We were a hell of a team together. Ray really set it out for Jerry and I. We got whatever we wanted. No questions asked." For the men responsible for watching Rayful's back no request was unreasonable. He was very generous and gracious in that way.

"People really liked Ray," Smoke says. "He could talk to people. Everybody wanted to be his friend. He was charming and mesmerized the girls." Edmond was a renowned lady's man and he often bestowed upon favored girlfriends oversize gold earrings that cost about $100 a pair. "He'd come in here and buy dozens of them for all those girls," the owner of a jewelry store on 14th

Street, Northwest said.

"Ray was like that with everyone." The D.C. hustler says. "If you just came home and went to see Ray he would hit you off. He would hit dudes off that just came home from jail and offer them a job." Edmond became a hometown hero; he made sure neighbors had turkeys on Thanksgiving and bought meals for the homeless, cars for his top staff and sponsored area basketball teams. He was like a black Don Corleone.

"When Rayful was in power everybody was getting money. People loved him, mainly because of his willingness to extend his hand. Times were extremely good for us financially. We slung coke on both of our main spots (M Street Northeast and Orleans/Morton Place Northeast) like a well-oiled machine. One spot sold mostly OZ's and under and the other sold the major weight. Our crew brought in a couple hundred thousand a week easily. Ray was a money making machine and he made sure the whole town ate good." Yo said. Ray was an avid basketball player and fan also.

Basketball was huge in the district, it was the neighborhood's relief valve and Rayful loved the game. He made sure that talented athletes who never made it to college, college stars who played at Georgetown University and drug dealers who played street ball got together to play tournaments. He was very involved in the basketball scene and culture in D.C. They still talk about Rayful's teams and tournaments today.

"Doctors play a round of golf to relax," said an Athletic League Supervisor. "Drug dealers play basketball." Ray was instrumental in the leagues, sponsoring a team in the Police Athletic League called *Clean Sweep*, the name of the police operation designed to get drug dealers off the streets. The stands were always packed with teenage boys and girls who came out to see Rayful and his team. They admired his sweet, arching jump shot and his joy-like exuberance when he played. Whenever Edmond's city league team played, the gym was full.

He enjoyed the company of Georgetown University's players such as Alonzo Mourning and John Turner, the 6-foot-7 forward that grew up with Rayful. "We certainly went to a lot of their games back in the day. Going to the games was pretty much like going most places in the city…a show. Going to Georgetown games was special because we had personal relationships with a lot of the players. Alonzo Mourning and John Turner were definitely two of the most notable players. Both were damn good youngsters. Zo dealt with Ray a little more, but JT was my main man. They would just hang and talk shit with us. We never involved them with any negative bullshit, out of respect, but some people had their theory anyway. They would both play on Ray's street ball team during the summer. Some college players and some street ball legends. Zo came to court a few times during our trial. Slim was a good stand up youngster. He did good for himself." Yo said.

Even though he was poisoning his community Rayful was an admired and respected man in the Chocolate City. He sought to give back to the community. Rayful said he loved the kids, and the impressionable poor children who lived near him, seemed to love him, believing him to be a celebrity. To them Rayful was the Robin Hood of the ghetto. They gawked at Edmond, his fabulous clothes, his glittery girls, his stylish cars and the famous basketball players who were his friends. In the Chocolate City, Ray was definitely the HNIC.

"We used to look out for damn near everybody in the neighborhood," Yo said. "Ray did a lot for people in our hood. We paid rent bills, bought school clothes for kids, paid hospital bills and even put food on some family's tables. If you were from our neighborhood and needed help in anyway, we made sure you and your family got it. We fed the workers every day and the neighborhood kids were always welcome to eat, while their families were at work. It was really safe in our neighborhood; we didn't allow anyone else to sell coke on Orleans and Morton Place. We had the whole strip on lockdown. We took in all the money around the clock 24/7." The whole crew was eating and Rayful's pockets were getting deep.

"I don't know if he was running shit back then, but everyone that was associated with slim was getting some bank, some more than others," D.C. Chris, a dude from the era says. With his flair and street persona, Rayful drew workers and admirers alike, by always traveling with an entourage and in cars like Porches or Jaguars. He was a walking employment advertisement. "Sell drugs, get money," was his company's motto.

"There goes Rayful and them, they getting it." People in the city said. "Slim was having shit his way," says Da Kid from Southeast. "I remember slim pulled up in my hood, and gave all us lil' niggas a $100 a piece and told us to take our lil' asses to school. I was like 7-years-old then and to me he was a star because he was getting out of a limo."

Edmond was 22 when his organization started generating enormous amounts of cash. With all the trappings that success brought, Rayful became a mythical figure in the downtrodden corner of the city he called home. He bought cars- Mercedes Benz's, Range Rovers,

BMWs- but the one that everyone loved the most was the white Jaguar with the gold hubcaps.

On a summer evening he would cruise around his hood in the white chariot like a knight in shining armor on his war steed and young children would run in his path worshipping the god of the ghetto. Rayful would shower them with $100 bills, basking in their adulation. He was generous in the manner of old style gangsters, handing out money, gifts, employment and advice. "He's a wonderful young man," a neighbor said. "I've known him and his family for years. He would make any parents proud."

In 1986, at the Florida Avenue Grill, which was on the corner of 11th and Florida, Rayful met Alta Rae Zanville, a middle-aged, white female that he befriended. The Florida Avenue Grill was where all the big hustlers ate lunch at. It was known as the capitals most celebrated southern food diner. It was also the home of a fencing operation run by the owner's sons.

On the way out of the restaurant Rayful saw Rae, as she was known, waiting for her Mercedes Benz to come out of the adjacent car wash. He had seen her in the restaurant selling jewelry out of a case. Her hair was bleached platinum blonde and shaved on the sides in a severe punk style. She wore a miniskirt slit up the side with stiletto heels. Rayful was attracted to her immediately.

"I know you're trying to make money," Rayful told her. He asked her if he could buy some jewelry. Rayful pulled out some cash and bought a gold ring from her. Then he gave the ring back to her, but let her keep the money. "Why did you do that?" She asked. "Because I like you and I don't need the money." Rayful said "Here's my number. Give me a call sometime." She would call him and the relationship would develop from there. Rayful was the first person who had been nice to her in a long time she said later, explaining how their friendship began.

Alta Rae Zanville was a 45-year-old woman who had been working as a clerk in the Navy for 26 years when she met Rayful Edmond. The meeting would prove fortunate for her. She was divorced and was drawn to the black social scene in the city. She hung out at popular clubs like the Foxtrappe on 16th Street near Dupont Circle. The forays into black culture took her closer to the edge, where she was comfortable. No one could understand their relationship though, due to the age difference.

Ray took a liking to Zanville immediately and started asking her advice in getting furniture, cars, etc. They became close friends. "Ray liked her," the D.C. hustler says. "Tony didn't like her. He was like why you fucking with that white broad? Ray was just a good dude. I didn't know what her position was. I just knew Ray was hitting her."

Rayful wasn't after her romantically though, sex aside. He needed her for business purposes. His drug dealing cash was piling up something fierce and he wasn't sophisticated enough to launder the cash through businesses or hide it in offshore accounts. Edmond just wanted to put his money into cars, apartments and houses for his mother and other family members.

But he didn't want his name on the cars or real estate, which would create a paper trail the law could follow. Getting Zanville to buy things for him would be better, Ray decided. It was a partnership that proved mutually beneficial. Zanville started renting apartments in her name for Ray. The first one was in Crystal City. Rayful paid Zanville $500 and the partnership was cemented.

Part 3

The Come Up

Nineteen eighty seven was Rayful's year on top. The demand for cocaine on the strip was so intense that Rayful couldn't keep up with it. His suppliers in the city couldn't hit him with enough yayo to keep his clientele happy. Rayful knew that if he could tap directly into a Colombian connection he could make more money than he ever dreamed of. The problem was securing that connection. With his need paramount, Ray devised a plan to go about getting a serious connect. He would let his flamboyancy speak for itself to secure him a connection. He knew if he put himself out there, the connection he needed would find him. Other than that he kept it low key and his crew kept it gangster. Rayful knew the only way to have a long run in the dope game was to attract as little attention as possible. But with the way Ray flossed, there was no way he was keeping it low profile.

"When we went out on the town, everyone showed mad love. People always wanted to get close to Ray when they were at the clubs. He was like a chick magnet; they came from all over trying to get a piece of slim. A few other youngsters that hung with him regularly had girls chasing them as well. Jerry and I often went places with the crew, but we stayed in the background scoping the scenery. If we went somewhere as a unit, most people either knew us or heard of us. I personally didn't like to be in the spotlight, so if you saw me that might not necessarily have been a good thing." Yo said.

Rayful was a mild mannered dude who wasn't confrontational, but his crew didn't mind bringing it, and for whatever reason. Rayful's view was there was enough money for everybody. The only color he saw was green and he ran his business to avoid bloodshed. He knew murders and conflicts were bad for business and only led to problems. Rayful avoided problems whenever possible. He liked to sidestep the drama and keep it moving. He let his team handle any problems or potential obstacles.

"We knew people were stealing coke and money, but Ray and Johnny couldn't see the things I saw. They were inexperienced when it came to seeing the wrong in people." Yo said. "They were still young and naive, because they both had good hearts and would give you the world if you asked for it. Me on the other hand, I wouldn't give you shit when it came down to business. If you worked you got paid. If you didn't, you had to move on, or get carried off by someone."

Rayful's crew was a family oriented drug ring and he kept his circle tight. "It wasn't no one big crew," Curtbone, a member of Rayful's crew said. "It was contractors. People freelancing." But they were all under Rayful, either directly or indirectly. He was the man who made it all go. Everything was done under his banner. "Curtbone was a youngster from Langston Terrace,

Northeast," Yo said. "He was a good soldier. Big boy was a well-respected youngster in all of D.C. Bone ran Langston Terrace with his crew. They were getting some nice paper on their own, but when slim started rocking with us, major loot came his way. Bone would come up to M Street and buy three or four joints and Ray would front him three or four. Bone moved up fast. He started getting 20 joints at a time. Our crew didn't have picks. We would front anybody. We knew one way or another the money would be collected."

Edmond's operation grew so fast that by 1987 he was making $1 million a week. "If you introduce Pepsi-cola into a new area, you're going to create a demand for something new." Eddie McLaughlin, a Narcotics Supervisor for the Washington office of the FBI said. "Edmond knew the potential for the market here. He was an early entrepreneur and he helped in its proliferation." Only in his early-20s, Rayful already had the biggest drug ring in D.C. But it was about to get bigger. Rayful was about to put his plan for securing a Colombian connect into play. "If you got good common sense, it'd tell you I'm up to no good." Rayful said. But Rayful couldn't have done anything or became an urban gangster street legend without his crew.

"Tony knew how to make things happen on a larger scale," Yo said. "Ray was very sharp also when it came to wheeling and dealing. I thought together we could take a big piece of Washington, D.C. for ourselves, and that's just what we did." As a whole the crew has gone down in infamy as one of the top drug organizations in the city. Rayful Edmond was the name, but the soldiers behind contributed their part and more so. The crew also styled and profiled, setting the treads rappers and Hollywood would later emulate.

"We wore all top flight shit. Ray would call one of his boys down in Georgetown, who would get us shit imported from their region." Yo said. "However, we started really stepping our gear up when Tony Lewis joined the organization. Tony was one of the best dressed dudes in the city. Ray and Tony would go on shopping sprees together buying all kinds of slick shit. The entire crew started rocking the likes of Hugo Boss, Valentino, Ralph Lauren, and the top of the line Versace shit...not that colorful lame shit.

"As far as cars, I personally was not a flashy-type of guy, but I did own a few Benz's, BMW's, Pathfinders, and a Mazda 929 when they first came out. A lot of dudes in our crew really didn't have to buy cars, because Ray had so many that they would drive, from BMW's, Mercedes', Range Rover's, Porches, etc. There were a number of clubs that our crew would hang out at. Mostly notably the Metro Club, Chapter III, and a few other spots that I can't remember at this time. We would often go to Atlantic City and Vegas to let our hair down as well." In April 1987, among the thousands of high rollers who converged on Las Vegas for the title fight between Sugar Ray Leonard and Marvelous Marvin Hagler, was an unusual delegation from Washington D.C. led by the flashy 22-year-old Rayful. The party included Zanville, Big Ray, Bootsie, Columbus "Little Nut" Daniels, Tony Lewis, Little Frank and a few others. They comprised Rayful's inner circle. The trip was taken in what would become Edmond's trademark style; a no expenses spared junket with only the best of everything.

The group flew first class and drove around Las Vegas in a white stretch limousine. Rayful was doing it big, trying to impress and attract attention. He put everyone up in separate rooms at the Imperial Palace Hotel and picked up all the meals and bar tabs. It was crazy. "As far as money, there wasn't no limit to him, he booked out 15 rooms, but we only used five, so people wouldn't complain about the noise," Curtbone said.

Rayful sported a gold chain around his neck with a gold medallion encrusted with diamonds. He had a $300,000 watch. Edmond loved boxing and often traveled to Las Vegas in a leased jet to watch his favorite boxer, Sugar Ray Leonard, demolish opponents. He took everyone shopping at the Gucci Store. His whole entourage was flossing with major style and bling. On fight night they watched Sugar Ray beat Hagler from $400 seats close to ringside. Of his inner circle Rayful said, "I would buy them cars, give them money, anything they needed." Money was spent like it was nothing.

"Our crew was tight back in those days, so like I said before, we would frequently visit Vegas and Atlantic City to party or to conduct some shopping. It was nice being on top, we would go to all the big fights no matter where they took place. The trips were unreal; we would be conversing amongst celebrities like we knew each other for ages. Professional ball players would gravitate to us more than anyone though. Ray and Tony Lewis would get complementary cards for everything, because they knew these two young brothers were going to gamble heavy. I saw them win and lose hundreds of thousands without breaking a sweat. I mean these dudes would be sitting there smiling after losing a few hundred large." Yo said.

Rayful was already a major figure in the D.C. drug trade, but the trip would prove to be a turning point in

Edmond's career. Edmond's entourage caught the eye of Melvin "Mel Dogg" Butler, a roving cocaine salesman from the Crips street gang in Los Angeles. The Crips dealt directly with Colombian importers and acted as middlemen in the cocaine distribution system in Los Angeles. Mel Dogg attended big fights for the precise purpose of finding men like Rayful; out-of-state, big city drug lords.

Butler was a matchmaker between drug retailers and West Coast wholesalers looking for new business. Butler checked out Edmond and recognized that he could be a conduit for his group to the lucrative Washington, D.C. market. On fight night, Edmond and Tony Lewis, had more to celebrate than Sugar Ray's upset victory. They were about to get plugged into the highest echelons of the cocaine trade. Through Butler, the two D.C. drug barons found what would be the ultimate California cocaine connection. A massive drug supply line that would funnel unprecedented quantities of white powder to the streets of D.C. "He wasn't as up as he was until he met those people out in Cali." The D.C. hustler says. "When he went out he got the connect. Then it was on."

Butler introduced Edmond and Lewis to Brian "Waterhead Bo" Bennett, a Crips' member who dealt directly with a Colombian supplier, Mario Ernesto Villabona. The relationship between Bennett and Villabona was perhaps the first between a Colombian and a member of a black street gang. Edmond was to become one of their best customers. He would go on to spend millions with the group.

"These guys showed us a lot of love when we did business with them," Yo said. "They were also some ruthless muthafuckas from Columbia, real big boys, so you had to come correct with these men. They knew it went the same way with us. We did business with the Columbians for four years, they were real good partners of ours."

Waterhead Bo and Mel Dogg would supply Rayful with unlimited quantities of white powder from Villabona. All Edmond had to do was bring the cash to L.A. and transport the bricks of coke back to D.C. Villabona was a wholesaler for the infamous Cali Cartel and he used Waterhead Bo to flood the streets of L.A. with coke. During the 18 months following the Leonard/Hagler fight, Edmond imported more cocaine into Washington than any drug dealer in the city's history.

"Rayful was a hell of a good man, back then. He would give you the shirt off his back if he befriended you. He was one of those types of young guys who knew how to get money. Ray loved to play and joke around all the time, but if someone mentioned the word money, his eyes and ears would open wide. He acted like a CEO of a major organization. He helped all of us get a major bank roll...but that was the Ray of the past!" Yo said.

The drug pipeline that fed Edmond was a graphic illustration of the reach of the global cocaine networks controlled by Colombian drug cartels, which supplied 80 percent of the coke imported to U.S. markets in the 1980s. The pipeline Edmond tapped into began in the valleys of the Andes and ended on the narrow, tree lined blocks of Northeast Washington, known as the strip, where Ziploc bags of cocaine sold for $50. With the new connect, Rayful made it snow in our nation's capital. The illicit proceeds generated from the flow of cocaine Ray imported were tremendous.

The streets of D.C. were literally covered in the white powder. Rayful created a snowstorm and was the original snowman on the East Coast. Young Jeezy was never in Rayful's class. Rayful was the drug lord who made it snow in D.C.

"When people saw Ray they saw flash and personality," D.C. Chris says. "I don't think he was feared or respected as an individual, but the dudes that were around him were respected and feared by many. That's how it's supposed to be. Everyone played their position." With enforcers like Yo, Jerry and Little Nut, Rayful was good. His crew acted as a team, everyone doing what they had to do.

Edmond avoided arrest because he dealt only with a small group of associates, and he rarely had contact with drugs or money. His inner circle was tight and nobody new was allowed in. With the Colombian connection out of L.A. Rayful started moving 100's of kilos into D.C. a month. He was doing it like Tony Montana in *Scarface*.

"It was like hitting the Powerball," says Smoke of the L.A. coke connection. The cocaine road to Edmond's distribution area in Northeast D.C. began in Cali, Colombia. From L.A., Rayful laid the groundwork for the large shipments of Colombian cocaine that hit the streets of Washington. It was a dream come true for Rayful, he was finally becoming the drug kingpin he always wanted to be. "He needed me and I needed him," Rayful said of his hook up with Butler. Butler had the drugs and Rayful had the money. It was a match made in drug dealers' heaven. An eventful meeting that Rayful had anticipated, planned for and exploited to his advantage. To Rayful it was fate and destiny. He was only getting what he had coming to him.

Rayful tested the network immediately. He dispatched Royal, his childhood friend, to L.A. with suitcases full of cash. Two million dollars for 200 kilos of high grade cocaine. Royal transported the coke back and held the kilos for Ray. Royal had graduated college with a degree in business administration, but he knew he could make more money with Rayful. It didn't take a college education to figure that out.

The coke would be brought in by U-Haul trucks and Ray's family would store up to 20 kilos at a time for processing purposes. Ray relied on them to bag and cut the coke. They were his in-house assembly line. Once he turned on the L.A. pipeline, Edmond ran a surplus at the strip and started to supply kilos to other major dealers across the city. He was seriously stepping his game up and becoming a major player in the drug trade on the East Coast.

Shipments of 200 kilos of coke were driven across the country in rented trucks or recreational vehicles. Smaller shipments of about 20 kilos were brought to the district in the luggage of couriers like Zanville and James Mathis, another friend of Rayful. When the shipments were driven, the drugs were often put into shipping cartons and packed aboard rental moving trucks. To avoid attracting attention to the trucks, because of their out-of-town license plates, drivers changed vehicles every other state.

At other times, the drugs were packed inside large recreational vehicles, which were not required to stop at truck inspection stations and on which out-of-state license plates aroused little suspicion. The couriers used similar ploys to reduce their chances of being spotted at airports. Couriers traveled with at least two large suitcases that were checked with the rest of the airlines baggage. The bricks of cocaine placed in the suitcases were surrounded with pillows to help foil security detection systems.

As one of Villabona and Waterhead Bo's largest customers, Edmond was alerted each time a major shipment arrived, usually about twice a month. Ray and several associates would fly to L.A. to negotiate the purchase of a large portion of the shipments. Edmond was paying up to $17,500 a kilo, but once it was cut and bagged for street sale, he was making 70 grand a kilo on the strip.

The West Coast distributors would negotiate only with Edmond, although underlings from both coasts would carry out the actual logistics of each cocaine purchase- carrying the money, delivering it to Mel Dogg or Waterhead Bo, and arranging for shipment to the D.C. area. The drug barons orchestrated the deals while their crews handled the actual operations of transporting the drugs.

An elaborate protocol extended to all business dealings. When Ray and Waterhead Bo met, they talked and partied, but money and drugs did not change hands between them. Edmond and Tony Lewis always arranged the delivery of the money to Butler, but they did not ferry the money to L.A. In an organization like this everybody played their position and guys like Rayful and Tony Lewis' roles were to lead.

Couriers who carried the cash for cocaine shipments flew to the West Coast before or after Edmonds personal entourage, but never on the same flight. When Edmond, Lewis and their personal aides dined in fine restaurants and made expensive shopping trips along Rodeo Drive, the couriers remained in their hotels until contacted by one of Edmond's key people. The person would then pick up the cash and deliver it to Waterhead Bo or Mel Dogg.

The couriers, who were paid $1,500 plus expenses for each trip to L.A., returned to D.C. immediately after delivering their caches of cash. Ray, Lewis and their entourage would return to the city after the purchase was completed. The drugs were delivered separately. It was all done with a business like precision. Unlike some of Villabona and Waterhead Bo's customers, Edmond always paid for his coke upfront. He trusted them to deliver the goods and he caught a nice break price-wise. With the L.A. coke hookup Rayful was finally in his element. His ambition of being a big baller was realized.

"D.C. was eating real good, because Ray and Tony Lewis had one of the best connects on the West Coast to feed us," Yo said. "Money was coming in from all over town. Crews everywhere were getting work from us. A lot of people who had the reputation as big boys in our town were buying from us or we were fronting them their work." With the West Coast connect Rayful had the Chocolate City on smash. Everything in the district ran through him.

Part 4

Balling

Rayful Edmond was a baller, as in world class baller. He put a lot of other dudes to shame. His flashy lifestyle made him famous on district streets and his cocaine empire generated $2 million a week at its 1987 peak. The flourishing business afford-ed its young executives a style of life well beyond their working class origins. And Rayful was president and CEO. "He ran D.C. He was hitting all D.C.," Smoke says. "He was bringing in millions of dollars." As the reigning king, Rayful was a man to be envied. He did everything first-class and carried himself like the ghetto superstar he was. In Dodge City Rayful was like a Hollywood celebrity. "I was real jazzy." Rayful said. "I tried to have a lot of class." Everybody wanted to be like Ray. He represented success and prosperity in the ghetto. "Everyday for two years I saw him give 20 grand away," Curtbone said. "On New Year's Eve he gave out 100 grand. Threw that shit on the ground. He'd fuck up 20 grand in sunglasses, then he'd give them out." And the man who didn't drink or smoke, would close down the streets around his

Northeast home to throw parties for the whole block.

"Ray's mother put together a cookout for all of us at her house in Maryland. She told everyone that she wanted to cook for all her sons." Yo said. "It was a big party, she sent out flyers and everything. The flyers read, *Come one, come all. A Spectacular night of wine, food and dancing for my sons: Rayful, Man, Tonio, Tony L., Jerry, Johnny, Red Jr. and Blue.* Ms. Bootsy was a thoroughbred. I've known this woman all my life and loved her like one of my aunts. She told stories of the times when we were kids." Rayful's crew grew up together. Their bonds were tight.

"Armaretta, Johnny's mother was the one in the family I most admired. The lady was all gangster. She didn't take any shit from no one. Johnny was one of my main men too, wild as shit, he kept some shit in the air, but could hold his own with the best of us. Johnny ran the M Street operation for us." Yo said. Edmond and his crew were said to have sold over 2,000 kilos of cocaine a week in the D.C. area. Many described him as more of a business man than a drug dealer. He headed an operation which ran hourly shifts and included multiple chains of command much like a Fortune 500 company. Rayful provided incentives and bonuses to his workers to insure loyalty and production.

The Edmond organization employed more than 150 people and his reach spanned across the country, with direct links to the drug cartels in Colombia. When his California connects, Waterhead Bo and Mel Dogg, came to Washington D.C. to visit and check out Rayful's operations, Edmond spent 50 grand in area stores on gifts for his visitors.

"Wherever I would go, I'd attract a lot of people,"

Rayful said. "I was real popular. People knew I had a lot of money. Everybody liked me and looked up to me." Life for Ray consisted of flashy cars like Mercedes Benz's, BMW's, Porsches and a Jaguar with gold inlaid hubcaps, and bling like a 45 grand Rolex watch on his wrist, 25 grand pendants, a three carat diamond stud in his ear and a 15 grand diamond covered cross around his neck. He took all expenses paid trips with his crew to the Super Bowl in San Diego, Mike Tyson fights in Atlantic City and Las Vegas title fights. Life with Ray was a non-stop party and good time. It was lifestyles of the newly rich and infamous. Being with Rayful was like being in a hip-hop video. Rayful was notorious for taking friends shopping at the pricey boutiques in Georgetown. Money was only a means to have fun for Ray.

"When we went shopping he gave me 10 grand to hold. Like it was nothing. He'd buy everybody he knew stuff." Curtbone said. One day Ray and a friend walked into Hugo Boss, the clothing store and spent 25 grand. He'd embark on 50K shopping sprees to New York, where he visited Trump Plaza and the Gucci Store. He once authorized a friend who was helping to furnish his house to buy 21 grand worth of furniture in a single month. In July 1987, Edmond handed a young friend 65 grand, so the kid could buy Edmond a new Porsche.

"We would go out to White Flint Mall or down to Georgetown Park Mall." Yo said. "Everybody started dressing fly as a muthafucka, even some of our youngsters were putting the pieces on, also the jewelry. Ray and Tony were in constant competition with each other, but it was a good thing between two friends.

"It was an ongoing joke with us all, Ray would get a Range Rover and then Tony would pull up with one too. And when Tony bought a new 560 sports Benz, Ray would get one too. They both went and bought the 560 Coup Benz together. We were all getting money, but those two young niggas were getting major paper. We went to all the big fights in Vegas and Atlantic City. The times were good and we had a ball."

Money flowed through Rayful's fingers like water. It didn't mean a thing to him. He spent it like it was nothing. Rayful would look out for his family too, especially his cousin, the up-and-coming gangster, Wayne Perry. "Rayful used to try to drop loads of shit down 203, but Wayne used to be like, 'Nah, I'm cool. I don't want nothing from you.'" Smoke says. Still Ray would look out for his cousin anyway he could.

Dom Pérignon champagne flowed at trendy nightclubs and the flamboyant dresser made cash purchases totaling $457,000 over two years from Linea Pitti, a pricey Italian men's boutique in Georgetown. And this was just on suits, clothes and $600 shoes. Rayful spared no expense and did everything first class. He spent money like Pablo Escobar and was charismatic like Muhammad Ali.

He would sit around for days counting money. His cash flow was seemingly endless. "My man told me that they was counting money." The D.C. hustler says. "Ray had money stacked up like three or four feet, it looked like a mattress. Like a bed you could jump on." In the chronicles of the drug trade Rayful has always been recognized and known as one of the big earners.

Edmond was a high roller, who loved to gamble at craps tables and play the numbers. He boasted of winning 100 grand in a single night. But Edmonds seemingly endless supply of money was not coming from gambling. His drug sales sometimes totaled $2 million a week. At his zenith, Edmond was controlling 60 percent of the coke coming into the city. "Ray was getting money." The D.C. hustler says. "But that was the era. It was love. Ray was supplying 90 percent of the city. It was all coming through Ray. Ninety percent of the coke was Ray's." His infamy transcended the drug game and saturated inner-city Chocolate City culture. He became a beloved figure. At the go-go clubs Rayful was getting mad love. The Rare Essence classic release, *Live at Breeze's Metro Club*, shouts out Rayful's name on one of the tracks. He was an iconic figure.

Rayful was a street star in D.C. and he loved his adoring fans. He wanted everybody to like him. He was a true ghetto celebrity. He wanted his limousine driver, Anthony Chaconas to like him. "I been over his house, ate over his house. We were great friends." Rayful said. When Edmond learned that Chaconas was behind on his bills, Edmond gave him money. "He treated me exceptionally well for a client." Chaconas said.

Edmond spent money at Beharry Jewelers on 14th Street too. "I'd go down there in the back of the store, go in the jewelry thing and take jewelry. He gave me jewelry. We was best friends." Rayful said. "Everyone that comes in my store is like a friend," Beharry said. "This is a business. I did business with Rayful. That's the truth." With Rayful showering money on the man's business they were the best of friends. Money had that effect. Everybody kissed Rayful's ass. He was the man in charge of the whole city.

Rayful Edmond made mind boggling sums of money in 1987 alone. "Between $35 to 40 million," he said. He swaggered through D.C. streets in fancy threads and expensive jewelry, always with a beautiful woman on his arm and 20 grand in his pocket. He attributed his position to, "just having a lot of street knowledge and being honest and putting a lot of work into it."

He dispatched couriers from Washington to California every three weeks with $2 to $3 million in cash to pay his cocaine supplier. With all the money he generated, the stick up kids must have been enticed, but nobody ever robbed Rayful. He was untouchable. He had too many wolves on his team. "Nobody ever did that," Ray said, talking about attempted jackings. He had a quiet and secure confidence. The self-assuredness of a man who knew he had a team of killers behind him to support his every move.

"We collected any money owed to Ray or our crew," Yo said. "Ray gave us a list and we were like mad hunters. We didn't care who was on that list, we were going to get that bank up off of you. Once Ray gave us your picture, we locked in on that and it was on, anywhere, anytime.

"Some guys thought they were real slick, but we had a few tricks up our sleeves too. They would be down at one of D.C.'s go-go joints, knowing damn well they owed money to one of the biggest crews in town. I used to help a lot of the beautiful young sisters in our neighborhood; you know money to get their hair and nails done. They would attend almost every one of Chuck Brown and Rare Essence's shows. We would show them pictures of the dudes we were looking for. Like clockwork they called with the information when we needed it."

Ray kept his team loyal by paying them well and buying them cars or even houses. Alta Rae Zanville and Royal Brooks, as Ray's confidants, started reaping a large profit. Rayful knew they could travel the country without attracting attention. Besides their monthly trips to L.A.

carrying millions of dollars, Zanville started her own high scale cocaine service to upper-class professionals and Royal started sending kilos down to North Carolina. Becoming a budding kingpin in the process.

Rayful had plenty of money, so he didn't mind. He had so much coming in that he once had $15 million, in denominations ranging from fives to hundreds at his house. He was generous with his money because he wanted to be. "I was just doing it because it was coming from my heart, that's how I felt," Ray said. He was the godfather of Dodge City.

"Rayful was very generous," a law enforcement official said. "He provided his people with the avenue to get all their acquisitions, it was the lure of money that made them turn a blind eye to the immortality of the drugs and death around them and embrace the business wholeheartedly." In the Chocolate City getting money was a way to survive, despite the depravation around them, Ray's crew thrived.

With the money flowing Rayful's family and friends ignored the effects of the coke storm on their neighborhood. They saw they were destroying their community but they ignored it. They exhibited their new found and ill-gotten wealth in full view of everyone. Ray flaunted his wealth to a degree that wasn't good for him. In the drug game jealousy breeds larceny. Ray wanted to be the man though and he wanted everyone to know. In retrospect his flamboyancy was his biggest downfall.

He thought he was on point. But in reality he was slipping. His eventual collapse was inevitable. Ray tried to play the game the right way. Despite his millions, Rayful had no bank accounts, checkbooks, ledgers, money orders, cars, houses or apartments in his name.

"That's the way the police, the way they would catch you," he said. But no drug kingpin of Rayful's status could ever go undetected or unnoticed and his actions would not go unpunished.

Law enforcement officials noted that the increase in cocaine abuse in the city closely tracked the period Rayful started taping into the Cali pipeline. "Slim made a grip," the D.C. gangster says. "It wasn't a problem or a factor for slim to be known for money getting. I can jive go for that." The king of cocaine was a folk hero to the city's youth, a modern day Lucky Luciano, who was worshipped in the streets of the Chocolate City.

"You know that with money, comes power and strength." The D.C. gangster says. "Ray had a crew of almost 200 working for him. He was powerful, and slim had folks that he fucked with that was very real men, so respect came with the territory. Dudes have respect for those who earn respect."

And with the Colombian coke connect, Rayful got an unlimited flow of the white powder, as did his cohorts. "He was from Northeast, but he was supplying a great portion of the whole city." Da Kid from Southeast says. With the kilos flooding the city, everyone was eating. Rayful's cocaine would fuel the coming crack era.

It's even said that Rayful acted as a cocaine liaison for other drug kingpins from New York like Alpo. Hooking them up with kilos, but clowning them in private. "He can't touch my money," Ray said of Alpo. "These niggas can't fuck with me. Touch $5 million cash." And Rayful was telling the truth.

"He had a ranch house in Maryland," the D.C. hustler says. "Ray had like a hardwood floor in the house and in the middle of the floor was a Jacuzzi and he could hit a button and the top would open and it was like five feet deep and it was full of money." As Rayful flooded the city and East Coast with cocaine his pockets were filled with cash.

At the height of his empire, Edmond became very friendly with several Georgetown Hoya players through his childhood friend John Turner. He loved the image of the Hoyas as black America's team, the first team of the hip-hop, inner-city youth era. He sat courtside at the Capital Centre for Hoya home games, always surrounded by his entourage and bodyguards. It was a D.C. thing, but he made it into a Rayful Edmond thing.

He relished the "12 angry black men" image of the Hoyas, often touting them as "Black America's Team" and the "First Team" of inner-city gangsters, thugs and hip-hop youth. Always cast as the dark, sinister and intimidating villain, the Hoyas made their way onto the court as the Georgetown band played the *Imperial March* from *Star Wars*, Darth Vader's personal theme song. Edmond would be seen smirking, shaking his head, laughing at and staring down the Hoyas opponents.

Edmond revered the tenacity, snarl and swagger the Hoyas played with, so much so that when his soldiers were gunned down, they were buried in Georgetown jerseys. Edmond became a fixture at Georgetown games, hobnobbing with John Turner and Alonzo Mourning. Alonzo and Turner would be seen riding around town in limo's with Rayful, going to clubs and playing on his teams in basketball tournaments at Barry Farms. It seemed everyone wanted to know him and every drug dealer wanted to do business with him. Most of his followers ignored his engagement in illegal activities. Ray was definitely the HNIC and king of the streets. But

Rayful was so high profile, he was attracting unwanted attention. With the money he was spending people took notice and they talked. Everybody knew what he did and what his business entailed.

When Georgetown coach John Thompson received news of what was happening in regards to his players hanging out with the drug lord he sent word to have Rayful meet him at his office at McDonough Gymnasium. He pleaded with Edmond not to hang around Alonzo, because he feared his chances of going to the NBA would be crushed. When Edmond tried to tell Thompson not to worry about it, that Mourning wasn't involved in anything illegal, the 6-foot-10 Thompson stood up and put his finger in Rayful's face. "Stay the fuck away from my players." The coach said. "Don't fuck with me." Rayful respected John Thompson, but only to a point. Mourning and Turner wouldn't betray their friends. Coach Thompson stayed on them. Turner eventually transferred to another college. He said Coach Thompson gave him a choice, "Quit hanging out with Edmond or get off the team." Turner said Thompson ordered him to leave because he continued his association with Edmond.

Part 5

Murder Capital

Washington D.C. will forever be known as the Murder Capital of the United States due to the drug violence during the crack era. The drug trade bred killers and Dodge City in the late-80s was a virtual war zone with bodies dropping on a daily basis. The shootouts, drive-bys and execution style killings were reminiscent of the brutal tactics used by Chicago gangsters in the 1920s. *The Washington Times* even ran a headline, *Gangland Killings in D.C. Emulate Capone-Era Style.* In February, under Rayful Edmond's watch, 13 people were killed by gunfire in a 24 hour period, a clear reminder of the Saint Valentine's Day Massacre in Chicago 70 years before, when seven henchmen of gangster Bugs Moran were shot to death by Al Capone's gun thugs. And like the Capone-era gun thugs, many of the crack era gangsters had huge egos, and boasted of their exploits after seeing them depicted on TV shows like the district's *City Under Siege.*

Crack hit D.C. in 1986 and its effects were immediate.

When crack became king, the streets of Chocolate City turned much deadlier. The police lost control of the neighborhoods and Washington became a Mecca for hustlers, enabling dealers to hold whole neighborhoods hostage. Terrifying the locals and applying an iron death grip on the drug trade. Rival dealers spilt blood, dying everyday for drug turf and spraying D.C.'s poor black neighborhoods with automatic gunfire, killing one another and painting the city red.

As crack tore through D.C. and people got hooked, crack babies, homelessness, carjackings, home invasion robberies, kidnappings, lost homes, lost jobs and families breaking apart became commonplace. Most of the drug dealers, drug users and victims of the drug related murders were young black men, and the young black man who came to personify the city's drug wars was Rayful Edmond.

"When crack hit the town all hell broke loose. People was doing whatever they could to have a chance to suck on that glass dick. It wasn't a good look for our town, but it affected the entire country the same way. Although, we benefited greatly from this epidemic due to us being one of the largest suppliers on the East Coast during that time." Yo said.

In 1986, when Edmond's cocaine business really took off, drug trafficking and drug related murders in Washington soared. Open air drug markets fueled the cities spiraling drug trade and grotesque hit man killings plagued the capital. It was a brutal world the district turned into. Honor was earned at the point of a gun. The young hustlers of the Chocolate City were not playing.

"Ray had some muthafuckas around him that would kill," Smoke says. "If Ray got in a verbal misunderstanding dudes would jump even if Ray didn't want that. Dudes would do shootings for Ray and Ray would get upset with them." In the hood it went from fistfights to guns in a New York minute. It wasn't until the mid-1980s that everyone in the drug business started packing a gun.

"One day these kids were in shoving matches," a detective said. "The next day they were in shootouts. They always wore black jumpsuits when they were going to shoot somebody." The escalation in violence, firepower and random bloodshed overtook the capital city toward the end of 1987 as a byproduct of crack taking over the streets.

The spasm caught city leaders totally by surprise. Some city officials argued that Washington was no different from other big cities besieged by crack and guns, but the violence proceeded with its own deadly logic for reasons of geography and even history that were unique to only the capital. In a city where politics juxtaposed with poverty the results were climatic.

"We have confiscated guns with silencers and with clips which hold 100 bullets," said D.C.'s police chief. "They have heavier firearms than the police carry." Crack and competition for sales bred violence and the body count started to rise from a low of 148 in 1985 to 197 in 1986 to 228 in 1987. Young black men were dying everyday and Rayful Edmond's organization was linked to many of the drug related homicides.

"We didn't care if it was daytime or nighttime, or if the person was at a grocery store, a barbershop or a nightclub." One dude from the era said of the mindset back then. "He could even be at a funeral and the preacher could be preaching, 'Thou shall not kill.' It won't make a difference because we'd kill his ass. Once the person was targeted, he might as well walk around with a big red bull's eye dot in the center of his head, because when its time for him to go, the bullet is going right through the skull." A deadly mentality took hold in Dodge City and the bullets began to fly. The Rayful Edmond crew wasn't taking no shorts.

"Everybody in this town knew if you owed Ray money and didn't pay, one day you would meet Tonio and Jerry and it was on our own terms, which way the hammer would fall." Yo said. "My partner Jerry has always been a real quiet man. It's almost an intense silence before the storm. I really don't know which one of us was the craziest. I would say he was crazier, because of some of the wild shit he did while we were putting in work on the streets.

"Everyone in our crew wore all black. This was part of our everyday attire. Black Champion hooded sweat gear. We had guns everywhere in our alleys. We were the two men most loved, hated and feared in the town of Washington, D.C. To me, being a thug in the enforcement game was a real challenge of one's mental and physical strengths. I had to stay on my toes 24/7 in this profession, because there's a lame around every corner who wants a crack at your title. You had to stay ready for war."

Members of Rayful's crew bragged that they used methods copied from both the Capone-era hitmen and from modern day ninja movies. Methods they used included setting dates for their victims' deaths and carrying out their slayings while dressed in hooded black sweat suits. As death and drug dealing ran wild on the streets, Washington D.C. became the new face and symbol of crack cocaine. Much to the politicians' dismay. But some members of the organization weren't with the killings either.

"Tony wasn't really with all that Ray was doing with the entourage, racks of people and the killings. He used to always tell Ray, 'You need to chill out. You need to holler at those little young 'uns.' Don't get it wrong, you fuck that money up, Tony would come see you. But Tony wasn't with all that." The D.C. hustler says. "He was more laid back with it, in the background. A real classy dude." But in the drug business, violence was a tool of the trade. A tool gangsters like Rayful employed to run their enterprise.

"We were on the big money paper chase, that's what kept Ray and Tony happy," Yo said. "Being an enforcer for the Rayful Edmond crew was hard work, because some of the people in our crew really didn't know the true meaning of loyalty. We had so many snakes in our midst and most of them were family or so called friends. Some of Ray's family members thought it was open season as far as them being able to come around and do little shit like steal. In their minds I guess they said to themselves, this is family, so I'm cool.

"Ray would have given anybody a helping hand. Ray was always on the move, trying to find a way to make our team more money, but sometimes one of those big butt young girls might have Ray hemmed up all day. Whenever Ray and Tony were around I went into protect mode. My first job was to make sure everybody stayed safe." With Yo and Jerry watching his back Ray could make his power moves.

Rayful Edmond was perfectly situated to take advantage of the crack age. His organization was as slick and well run as McDonald's. Morton and Orleans

Place became so crowded that on some days Edmond's lieutenants had to order customers to form lines that stretched 100 buyers long. People in the hood and the suburbs were fiending for crack.

Rayful sat atop an organization of nearly 200 employees that moved an estimated $20 million worth of cocaine and crack a month from Colombia via the Crips. He controlled 60 percent of the city's cocaine market, and the market was growing because of crack, the most destructive drug in the city's history. The emergence of crack created many problems. Chaos being the foremost.

Cracks effects were immediate. The drug left its mark on the whole narcotics economy and helped a whole new class of entrepreneurs show their marketing ability. When crack started, Rayful lost control; the epidemic was good for business, but bad in other ways. Washington, D.C. became known as the Murder Capital of the World because of the drug violence that erupted during the crack era.

D.C. soldiers went so hard that they even had territorial beefs with those outside their zones strictly on G.P. "You didn't want to get caught hustling in Southeast if you was from Northeast. You just couldn't do that. It could get you killed." Smoke says. Money, mayhem and murder ruled the day, this was what the game was about. The coming of crack created drug tycoons in D.C., albeit, destroying the community in the process. And Rayful was the top dog.

"He's the Babe Ruth of crack dealing," U.S. Attorney Eric Holder said of Rayful Edmond. "The youth of this city know more about Rayful Edmond than great civil rights leaders." His popularity was on blast, but Rayful had his mind on money. He had that "get money" attitude. He was hustling everyday way before Rick Ross wrote the hustling anthem.

Money was the means to all ends in the city and in Rayful's eyes he was just providing for his family. With an endless cash flow he was able to attract lots of beautiful women, the company of well-known athletes, and provide for his family and friends fueling his popularity as well as helping his people buy the material possessions they desired. It was all just a lifestyle to Rayful.

So what if people all around were getting hooked on coke and crack babies were being born to tortured lives? So what if narcotics dealers were spraying D.C.'s poor black neighborhoods with automatic gunfire, killing one another? Edmond didn't see himself as responsible. It was business and business for him was great.

"People get killed, people lose their jobs, people get strung out. A lot of my friends from my neighborhood lost their lives because I brought drugs into the community." Rayful said. "Some babies probably was born from crack because of me. I feel bad about it now, but back then I was just thinking of power."

In his pursuit of power, Rayful became wrapped up in a brutal drug war. "The drug trafficking took on a life of its own." Curtbone said. "People was affiliated with Ray, but he had no control." The lucrative drug trade caused turmoil, it was like the Notorious B.I.G. said, "More money, more problems."

In this time period, police said Rayful's ring was responsible for multiple murders. Rayful didn't have any control of the murders or who got killed insiders claimed, but the murders brought attention to the whole enterprise. As the front man and leader of the crew, the blame lay at Rayful's feet.

Ray was ultimately responsible in law enforcement's eyes, because he was the head of the organization. All the tentacles reached back to him. But dudes in the street knew different. They knew how and why it went down and they have defended Rayful to this day. It was the gun thugs causing the havoc, not Rayful.

"Ray was the mediator always." Curtbone said. "'Let 'em get that little bit of money. That won't hurt me.' He said." But Rayful's crew had a different attitude. They were ready to pull the trigger. Anything that encroached on their territory was a threat.

"We were thugs of enforcement and our main job was protection against any and all situations that Ray or Tony might see or not see. Our job was very easy when it came to Tony Lewis, because he wasn't going for shit. You couldn't get past slim with that bullshit." Yo said. "Tony Lewis was never the friendly type. Tony was on top of his game 100 percent, but Ray had this thing about him.

"He wanted to be respected by the older players in our town. He didn't really need to go about it that way, because everything in town went through his hands. Everybody in town knew Ray was one of the major money makers, but they also knew he was a little green when it came to understanding the motives of some people. A lot of people came at him with that 'I'm your friend' shit. Ray ate that up. He loved that kind of attachment with the streets. Johnny would always tell him about being so damn gullible."

Trinidad was on the city's East Side, sandwiched between Florida Avenue and H Street. It was a compact neighborhood of narrow streets and brick row houses named for the ten block street that ran through it. It was a prime drug spot just to the east of the two narrow, one

66

way streets of Orleans and Morton Place, where Rayful's open air drug bazaar was located. When a rival crew set up shop in the Trinadad section Rayful was infuriated, and so was his crew.

"I wasn't too surprised when his crew went down, because they were doing a lot of back and forth beefing prior to his arrest." D.C. Chris says. Early in 1988, the taunting and fistfights between the two crews escalated into gunfire. In June, shooters from the Trinidad faction drove to Orleans Place and gunned down Leslie "June" Wheeler and Anthoney "Mad Dog" Thomas.

An immediate answer was necessary from Rayful. No retaliation would have left him looking weak in the eyes of the streets. And this Rayful couldn't abide. He had an organization to run and a reputation to uphold. The streets were watching. Show weakness and the sharks would smell blood. The streets demanded an eye for an eye, Old Testament style. Respect was paramount.

"The Trinidad crew had some real good soldiers within the ranks," Yo said. "I sent a crew of hitters to the Trinidad area. They came back and said it looked like a ghost town. A few of the Trinidad guys came at us and aired it out with twenty or thirty rounds of ammunition. They drove by and shot one of the youngsters in the leg. When we got the news that one of the kids in the neighborhood got hit I knew it was time to bring the pain."

After midnight on June 23, 1988, Edmond and a few of his crew went to Chapter III, a nightclub on First Street, Southeast. Rayful came with his lieutenant and enforcer Columbus "Little Nut" Daniels, a short teenager with close cropped hair and a smooth babyface, who wasn't afraid to pull the trigger. His short stature pushed him to be the big man. And for Little Nut, that meant letting his gun do the talking.

"Lil' Nut was a cold blooded killer, who looked like a kid, but he was an animal with that banger. His job assignment was given to him directly by Ray, but it was really me who told Ray to keep shorty with him at all times. Shorty kept his banger with him and wasn't afraid to use it. Lil' Nut was a true thug in the enforcement game and Ray would be safe while he was roaming through town. His first and last job was to keep Ray safe." Yo said.

Rayful and Little Nut bumped into Brandon Terrell, a member of the Trinidad faction. Edmond warned Terrell to stay on his side of Florida Avenue but Terrell told Rayful, "Fuck you." Rayful didn't react, but when Terrell left the club, Little Nut followed. In the parking lot he drew his gun on Terrell, who started to run, but it was too late. Little Nut put two bullets in Terrell's back, which dropped him. Then Little Nut stood over him and pumped in five more rounds. When Little Nut fled to celebrate the hit with Rayful, Terrell bled to death on the asphalt.

"Lil' Nut had to bang his gun in front of three or four hundred people down at the Chapter III night club," Yo said. "A wild youngster from Northeast pulled his gun out on Ray and Lil' Nut talking crazy, showing off in front of this brother from Northwest D.C. named Fraybean. The youngster fired in the direction where Ray and Lil' Nut stood.

"Nut told Ray to get down and stay down. Shorty jumped up, gun in hand and ran right at his man. He banged off about five or six shots. The youngster had this surprised look on his face when he saw Nut running at him with his 9mm in hand, blazing fire from its barrel.

"Shorty always carried that fifteen shot 9mm and that muthafucka was spitting hot leaded saliva that night. Some people don't understand our lifestyle; they say all kinds of bad things about how we make our money and conduct our business. But that night when Lil' Nut fired his pistol, he not only saved his life, he saved the life of one of his friends.

"Lil' Nut fired his banger to protect himself from bodily harm. In the United States of America they call that self-defense. The youngster that left us that summer night in front of the night club was named Brandon. He made a name for himself in the mean streets of Washington, D.C. by putting a few people to sleep permanently. Brandon was a gunslinger himself, but that night he forgot the rules of engagement. If you pull it, make sure you use it until complete termination."

Edmond's top enforcers, Jerry Millington and Antonio "Yo" Jones knew that the Trinidad crew would retaliate for Terrell's shooting. They sent Greg Royster to a gun shop in Virginia Beach and he returned with a small-cache of semiautomatic weapons and submachine guns. Millington and Yo arrayed them on a blanket in the alley behind Orleans Place and called roll.

"The drug game is like one of those soap operas we see on TV, because things can change fast. New players come up from nowhere. We were in a constant battle over the area's terrain." Yo said. "Jerry and I would go to the shooting range twice a week. We worked out once a week with blades. One of my older brothers was a war hero. He knew all about hand to hand combat. I asked him to show Jerry and I some knife fighting techniques."

Edmond's trusted gang members filed in with military discipline and were assigned weapons. They were ready for war. "The thing about that beef," the D.C. hustler says. "Ray told them to come out to Maryland. You couldn't even stand on the street. They was killing. That shit was crazy. It was like a ghost town in the city. No one was going out until that was resolved."

Rayful wanted to reward Little Nut for killing Terrell. Edmond gave Zanville 51 grand cash to buy Little Nut a Mercedes Benz 300 CE. It was a dark blue beauty and Little Nut drove it through the strip slowly a few times just to make sure everyone saw his trophy. But he had to be careful. He couldn't flaunt his trophy bought with blood money like that.

The Trinidad faction was out for blood. It wasn't safe on the strip or in the hood. The beef turned the Chocolate City into a war zone. Dudes were packing heat and weren't afraid to bust loose. "Niggas was dying in the street every day," Smoke says. "Dying for blocks they didn't even own. Dying for the right to sell poison to our people."

In August, at a Maryland seafood restaurant, a D.C. homicide detective slipped into a chair across the table from Rayful. "Give us Little Nut," the detective told Rayful. Edmond, flanked by two tables of associates, responded in a polite and measured tone that Little Nut was a "real good friend of his." He did not know whether he committed the slaying, but he would "see what he could find out about it."

Edmond's answer came less than 24 hours later, in the form of a 16-year-old youth who arrived, with his mother, at homicide headquarters, with a confession to make. He, not Little Nut, was responsible for Terrell's killing. Peppered with questions from two detectives, the boy's story quickly fell apart.

The youth, whose mother had picked him up that morning at Edmond's house in Northeast, acknowledged that he lied, later telling authorities that Edmond had persuaded him to take the fall for Little Nut because as a juvenile, he could be sentenced to a maximum of two years and his family would be supported during his detention.

The detective picked up the phone. "Nice try," he said to Edmond. "But we still want Little Nut." Rayful thought he could manipulate his way out of any situation. He thought he was clever like that and could outsmart the cops at their own game. Despite his success, Rayful was naïve in a way.

"It was the power he had." A detective said, describing why a youth would agree to almost certain incarceration for a crime he did not commit. Ray was seen as a god like figure in the city. His word was law and he was so nice, charismatic and gentleman like in his requests, which were backed by large sums of money that he was rarely, if ever denied.

Another time when a detective tried to serve Rayful with a grand jury subpoena in connection with the shooting, Edmond arranged to meet the detective at a certain time on a street corner. "Exactly at that time, Rayful pulled up in a white stretch limo with a driver," the detective said. And when he went to the grand jury, he brought his lawyer Arthur Reynolds, who was known to battle for his clients fiercely, with him. Rayful did not take any chances. Everything he did was well thought out for effect. Rayful always played with the better hand, but his luck was about to run out.

With the law circling, the streets took their own form of justice. As Rayful and Little Nut were sitting side by side in a neighborhood barbershop getting a shave, two men walked in wearing ski masks. They pulled guns and shot Little Nut point blank in the chest, spine and abdomen. Little Nut wasn't killed, but he was paralyzed from the neck down. He would never drive the blue Mercedes again.

A month later police walked into Little Nut's hospital room and charged him with killing Brandon Terrell. In the drug game most players end up dead or in prison. That is just a fact of life. With so much killing and shooting it was beginning to affect business. The bottom lines were suffering. The crews couldn't make money and something had to be done, one way or another. With the law was all up in Rayful's affairs, he knew he had to call a truce before things got deadlier and more police got involved.

"When Rayful's crew had its issues with the dudes from Trinidad and bodies were dropping all over the city, dudes turned to Fray." Smoke says. Michael Fray or Fraybean was a street legend in D.C. "Rayful called me and Jerry after the guy talked to him for over an hour about the situation with the Trinidad crew. The brother who made the call was Fray." Yo said. "Rayful used to kick it with Fray sometimes, so he thought they were cool. We knew it was always about what Rayful could do for him financially.

"Fray was losing too much money with the Trinidad crew off the streets in hiding. They bought their pack from Fray, so if Fray didn't make any money uptown moving the shit he had, then he would have come up short financially. Fray asked Ray to put together a sit down, so we could squash the beef with the Trinidad crew."

Law enforcement later identified Michael "Fray" Salters as the person who, in August 1988, imposed a cease fire in the bloody warfare between Rayful's crew and the Trinidad faction. "Michael Fray squashed that." The D.C. hustler says. In the last week of August, Rayful, Tony Lewis and their rivals met in a schoolyard near Howard University to squash the beef.

"Rayful called us and said they wanted to meet on the football field of Banneker Junior High School on Georgia Avenue, Northwest. Rayful and Tony Lewis walked to the field with about ten men fully armed with 9mm pistols. All of our other men had Israeli machine guns," Yo said. "Fray and his nephews walked up along with the Trinidad crew. The meeting started with Rayful talking with Fray and then Tony Lewis walked over. They all shook hands and started to talk. Rayful and Tony called Jerry and I over to talk. They wanted to hear it from us that the beef was over." With the whole Rayful Edmond crew in agreement a truce was called.

"Fray was paid 100 grand by Rayful to put an end to that. Fray had power like that." Smoke says. But Yo, who was there, disputes that. "I've read somewhere in a street magazine that we supposedly paid Fray a large amount of money to put together a big meeting between us and the Trinidad crew." Yo said. "I couldn't do anything but laugh over that. Fray owed the Rayful Edmond crew close to 90 grand. The youngsters in the Trinidad crew were his main source of income, so as long as the beef was on he was coming up short. That's the real reason behind the meeting. We agreed to the meeting for the same reason."

The truce didn't last. Less than two months later Gregory Cain and Ronald Curry, the suspected Little

Nut shooters, were sitting in their car on the 800 block of K Street, Northeast in Trinidad. Yo and Millington, according to police, ran up from behind, flanked the car and fired through the window from both sides, allegedly killing the occupants. That's just how it went down in the Murder Capital.

Part 6

The Heat is On

In May 1988, Edmond's elaborate, cash rich, corporate style drug operation started to crumble when four men were arrested in Los Angeles for offering an undercover officer $1 million for a cache of coke. Eventually the men began to talk and the man they talked about was Rayful Edmond. By the late-80s the feds had Rayful clearly targeted. He was an iconic figure and the feds wanted to show the streets that nobody was above the law. Rayful brought a lot of violence, terror and drama to the D.C. area and law enforcement was sick of it. His crew turned the city into the Wild, Wild West and police linked his gun thugs to multiple homicides. There was some serious Billy the Kid-type of gunplay going on and the powers that be weren't having it. It was time to put an end to Rayful Edmond, the feds decided. With the crack era in full swing, D.C. was out of control with gun violence, new jack gangsters and drug trafficking. It wasn't a good look for our nation's capital. As the power play of national politics played out in the media, behind the scenes an atmosphere of blatant gangsterism was emerging. This was something the authorities couldn't abide. In the midst of the chaos, to law enforcement's benefit, Edmond's organization began to unravel.

In Missouri, a van doing 68 mph in a 55 mph zone was pulled over. Suspicious that the driver was from California, although the van was registered in East St. Louis, the officer searched the vehicle. Underneath a mattress were 20 cartons filled to overflowing with cocaine, 1102 pounds of it, all professionally wrapped into bricks marked in undecipherable code. Some were stamped with a small scorpion, symbol of the Cali Cartel, the Colombian drug trafficking organization that was supplying Edmond's network.

It was the second largest seizure of cocaine ever made in the United States and it would lead law enforcement officers to establish direct links between Waterhead Bo, Mel Dogg and Rayful Edmond. Federal investigators were able to trace an unbroken chain of transactions over an 18 month period in 1987 and 1988, that brought cocaine from processing plants in Colombia through Mexico into Los Angeles and across the country to D.C. Edmond's cocaine pipeline was exposed and the feds were ready to take him down.

The methods used to supply Edmond's organization illustrated the meticulous and increasingly sophisticated way drug traffickers used the nation's highways and airports to transport massive quantities of cocaine. During the year-and-a- half that the L.A. to D.C. drug pipeline was in operation, a highly organized transcontinental supply system operated with virtual impunity, thwarting the best efforts of federal and local law enforcement officials.

Authorities believed that in early 1988 Edmond was buying more than a quarter of all the cocaine the Cali Cartel was shipping into the United States. Waterhead Bo and Mel Dogg may have been making as much as $1.5 million in profits from their weekly delivers to Edmond. "The middleman made a killing on this." A DEA agent said. But they weren't stacking it. In typical drug dealer panache, the money was spent freely. Easy come, easy go. Another day, another drug deal.

The pipeline ran smoothly, but eventually things got hectic due to mismanagement and circumstance. Ray's haphazard management techniques belied his cool and calm precision. His unraveling as the pressure mounted affected his casual business manner. A plethora of problems arose. Edmond often recruited couriers at the last minute, delaying transactions. Sometimes the suitcases full of money were too heavy for the couriers to carry and Edmond would have to find more couriers. Along with the busts it became a never-ending drama. A D.C. soap opera with Rayful as the centerpiece and star.

In April 1988, two female couriers headed back to D.C. after dropping off several hundred thousand dollars in cash and were stopped at Los Angeles International Airport, when Los Angeles police officers recognized them as having arrived from the East Coast about an hour earlier. In the ensuing confrontation one of the women was arrested for assaulting an officer. She went all out ghetto on the officer, drawing unwanted attention to Ray's organization.

On a trip taken January 11, 1988, Edmond, Royal Brooks and a few others flew from D.C. to L.A., where they met Mel Dogg. Edmond and Butler obtained approximately 200 kilograms of cooked cocaine then packaged it in kilogram lots. They delivered the drugs to a mobile home that Edmond said was bound for D.C. The cocaine never made it. By theft, bust or carelessness, Rayful was losing shipments. This was costing him an undetermined amount of money, possibly in the millions.

On the home front things were getting hectic also as the investigation around Rayful heated up. Every department of the law was anxious to close in on Edmond. In early 1988, police executed search warrants on abandoned houses at 635 Orleans Place, 656 Orleans Place and 642 Morton Place. These were stash houses for the strip and police found a total of 300 grams of cocaine and 400 grams of cocaine base, thousands of dollars in cash and nine firearms.

After the search police saw Yo and Millington watching four other people clean up the 656 Orleans Place house. "We would sometimes keep small amounts of money or coke in some of the backyards." Yo said. "That way if the police did catch one of our lieutenants in the alley he wouldn't have a lot of cash in his pockets. The cops would steal money or drugs, and crack heads would steal anything that wasn't nailed down."

During a February 18, 1988 search, police observed Keith "Cheese" Cooper, who had been supplying sellers in the 600 block of Orleans Place when police arrived, throw down $1,400 in cash. "Cheese knew how to keep the youngsters real busy." Yo said. Police recovered 100 $25 bags of cocaine in a plumbing pipe in the basement of the house as a result of another search. They were onto Edmond's enterprise, the strip was getting hot.

Aware that their phones might be tapped, members of the crew grew very wary of what they said over the phone and of which telephones might be used. Bootsie expressed concern that her phone and those of family members were being tapped. She called Rayful from her office where she was not afraid the phone lines were being tapped. Reminiscent of *The Wire*, a lot of conversations were caught on tape.

Rachelle Edmond told Rayful not to call her portable phone because it was "hot as a firecracker." She changed her phone number numerous times out of paranoia. Despite the investigation Rayful carried on, business as usual. No one could tell he was shook due to his ice cold and charismatic outer façade. But he was taking tremendous losses and his family and crew were becoming increasingly paranoid.

"We started to get all kinds of heat from phone taps to surveillance," Yo said. "Things were starting to fall apart fast. The feds raided one of my spots and took a substantial amount of money. People started to look at us funny, as if they knew our time was coming to an end."

In late April, Edmond sent Royal Brooks to L.A. with more than $3 million in cash to buy 200 kilos of coke. Except there was none for sale. Waterhead Bo couldn't come up with anything. Edmond pushed on with Mel Dogg's help. He and Rayful lined up two L.A. drug dealers to help look for cocaine, but the results were disastrous.

One of the dealers, John Watts, took an undercover cop posing as a supplier, to the house where the money was being stored. A short time later, authorities seized almost $2 million from the house. Watts didn't make the connection and he contacted the same undercover officer to buy the 200 kilos. Edmond had more cash delivered from the district.

"As you know all good things must come to an end, but shit really started to go bad when we lost roughly two million in cash out in Cali. Ray sent a few dudes out to Cali to re-up on coke when they got fucked around in some sort of drug sting conducted by the DEA. The shit happened in a parking lot of a restaurant called the 'Proud Bird' or some shit like that. My partner and I immediately flew out there to find out what the fuck was going on with our buy money. We started to get heat about a number of random shit. As soon as we got back in D.C., the DEA generated a task force designated to get us off the streets. These muthafuckas set up shot right around the corner from our main distribution area, shit was getting real serious." Yo said.

The delivery took place on May 5, 1988 in the parking lot of the Proud Bird, a chicken restaurant a few blocks from Waterhead Bo's headquarters. But the cocaine wasn't coming from him. It was being supplied by the L.A. Sheriff's Department. Everything went as scheduled. Watts handed over $1 million in cash and an associate took the 200 kilo delivery. They were arrested with Brooks and Mel Dogg. They seized another $1 million Brooks had on hand to complete the deal.

"That was Ray's man." Smoke says of Royal. "He got locked up trying to make a move. Ray was fucked up. He was upset." The cops got the $2 million in the house and then got another $2 million Rayful had sent out with Zanville in the sting. It was a good day for law enforcement. Fighting the War on Drugs was their calling. They were happy with the cash, but wanted more. They wanted all the culprits in the affair.

"Our main man Melvin set up a big deal for us. It should have been a sweet move, but the fucking feds

confiscated just a little under 1.2 million of our money."
Yo said. "That shit hurt big time, because three weeks
prior to that the local police department in L.A. raided
one of Melvin Butler's houses and beat us for two million
cash."

James Mathis was one of the couriers that got busted
with the drugs. He flipped and agreed to cooperate
against Royal and Rayful. Mathis had flown to D.C.
about eight times with suitcases full of kilogram-sized
bricks of cocaine. He knew the inside details on Rayful's
organization and told it all. "They took four million
dollars and flipped Mathis," Smoke says. "A week later
Ray sent three more million." Rayful was a cash king,
his pockets were deep.

"Ray called a meeting and we all got together, we
needed to put together some cash real fast." Yo said. "The
meeting consisted of Ray, Tony Lewis, Jerry, Johnny,
Curtbone, Red Jr., Armaretta and me. The meeting was
all about money. Ray and Tony wanted to know who had
what to put in the pot so that we could make a quick
move for about 200 keys of coke. I put up 200 grand,
Jerry matched my money, Johnny put up 100 grand,
Armaretta gave 80 thousand, Red Jr. put in 50 thousand
and Curtbone put up 170 grand. Ray and Tony put up
600 grand a piece, which brought us up to 2 million.
This time Jerry and I were sent out west to keep an eye
on the cash."

The losses mounted but Rayful got to a point where he
couldn't stop. He said, "I'm in it too deep." Whatever he
had to do to keep it going he would do. When it ended
he knew an indictment was coming. He just wanted to
make as much as he could until then. But all types of
things were going wrong. He realized that his phone

calls were being intercepted. The government had placed wiretaps on Edmond's phone and were recording all his phone conversations.

Rayful was recorded telling Butler he'd send "three or four million," and Butler referred to Edmond as "my partner." Also an unidentified man telephoned Edmond to report that, "Whitey got the dude around here now," and to ask whether he should "give it to him." Edmond told the caller to give the man "the half."

Raynice Thompson carefully chose her words, so as to not utter the word cocaine or a frequently used code word for cocaine, over the telephone. Instead, she would tell Kathy Sellers that, "I am ready for you" or that, "I have something for you," to refer to Sellers picking up cocaine that was ready to be delivered to the strip.

On one occasion Raynice Thompson telephoned Sellers to tell her that George Derricott would be "dropping the package off." Rather than have Sellers pick up cocaine from their Oak Crest Towers Apartment, Raynice and Jeffrey Thompson would meet Sellers at night near a junior high school, because it was deserted in the evening hours.

"Ray just got too big, too fast. You just knew the feds were gonna come get him," Mr. T says. The arrests of his couriers and street dealers hastened his downfall and Rayful knew it was coming. "He'd be playing," Curtbone said. "We going to jail." He acted gleeful and playful, but Rayful was tense as his organization members were picked off one by one. It was a very trying time for the crew that was used to being on top. Rayful was concerned about Royal who had taken the fall in the deal gone wrong.

"Jerry and I received a phone call from Ray." Yo said. "He was very concerned about his friend Royal Brooks safety. Rayful talked for about an hour about this lame-ass nigga. We knew Royal was weak as shit from day one, but that was our man's friend so we let him handle all those lames he fucked with. We just told him to keep them punks away from men like us. Rayful respected our wish and didn't bring his buddies around us.

"Ray wanted us to go to the City of Angels, Los Angeles, California. He put together a meeting with Melvin Butler and a few more heavy hitters from Cali. The meeting was concerning keeping this punk Royal safe on the inside. Melvin had a strong team on the inside, we called them The Big Blue Wrecking Crew.

"The fuck boy Royal was calling home everyday crying like a little bitch. Ray got tired of him crying. He said, 'Royal sounds really scared over the phone and I don't think he can hold out any longer.' So I said, 'Let's cut our ties with him now.' We wanted Melvin to get a few of his brothers on the inside to put a knife in the lame-ass nigga, but that wasn't our call to make. Ray was soft on issues of this nature.

"We found out they were carrying Royal like a real bitch. Those guys in the block had Royal washing underwear and doing their hair every night. They used to play sex games with Royal. He was a bitch slap away from getting butt fucked. We told Melvin to get on top of keeping the lame safe. That's what Ray wanted." Yo didn't like Royal and he wasn't too hot on Alta Rae Zanville either.

"I had very little contact with the broad Alta Rae Zanville. I focused on making sure our security and defense mechanisms were in order. That hot bitch came around Ray's family mostly. I saw her a few times in passing, but I didn't need any new friends, so I always

Rayful Edmond

kept my distance from outsiders. I knew a little bit about the fuck boy Royal Brooks. I know Ray took care of that piece of shit…money, cars, tuition for school, etc." Yo said.

Kathy Sellers had been heavily involved in the Edmond organization and was the former girlfriend of Yo. She started cooperating and told how under the direction of Millington she began picking up bags of cocaine in the fall of 1987. Later, she received drugs from David McGraw and drove them to the strip for delivery to Millington, Cooper, Monford, Jones and others.

She made deliveries until the early summer of 1988 and was paid $800 per week. She held packages for the organization that would later be picked up and taken to the strip by James Minor. Sellers picked up money from sales on the strip also, collecting up to 10 G's at a time and delivering it to Millington's house in Upper Marlboro, Maryland.

With informants running rampant and law enforcement investigating the scene it was getting hot in the city for Rayful's crew. Just how they did the Mafia, the feds started following him. Rayful would wave at them. He said, "I'm not gonna run, I'm not gonna hide. I'm just gonna face it." But Ray had some serious misconceptions about his criminal behavior.

"Ain't nobody got nothing from me." He said. "If they never catch me with drugs in my hand, I'll never go to jail." Those were old school principals handed down to him by his parents and uncles, but in the late-80s War on Drugs culture they no longer applied. With the conspiracy laws and mandatory minimum sentences the feds had enacted, they had a lot of tools to go after Rayful and his crew. All the alphabet boys were getting in on the act and trying to get a piece of the action. Rayful's family and confidants started to express concern that they would be questioned, that their homes would be searched or that their financial transactions would be scrutinized. In a conversation with Atla Rae Zanville, Rachelle Edmond told Zanville what she would say if law enforcement officials questioned her about Rayful.

She told Zanville that it would be a good idea to destroy anything that she had with "other people's names on it" and that she had "burned every damn thing." She also told Zanville that, "I stopped even writing checks for my bills. I started getting money orders and tearing the receipts up." Rachelle was not the only one who feared law enforcement officers would find incriminating evidence in her home. Raynice had a similar fear, which caused her to stop holding cocaine at her home. Bootsie went to great pains to make sure her financial transactions did not look suspicious. Even when she had extra money, she paid off the same amount on her debt to the IRS each month, because as she said, "When you start paying off a whole lotta things, first thing they wanna know is where the money came from."

The feds had surveillance and wiretaps on the whole crew. They were gathering all the evidence they would need. They were building a case against Rayful one piece of evidence at a time. Things were getting so hot that Rayful couldn't even get any product. "Our friends out west were getting a lot of heat from the DEA, so they had to put us on hold again." Yo said.

Rayful was not without his own means of gathering info. He had a captain and lieutenant from the D.C. Metro Police in his pocket. There were a lot of leaks making their way to him concerning police raids, who got busted and who was snitching on him. Rayful paid a lot of police to do a lot of stuff for him, be it getting info, tipping him off or guarding drug shipments or stash houses. "A Lieutenant Mitchell was giving Ray all kinds of information to help us get around his co-workers," Yo said. With dirty cops on his side Rayful extended his run a little longer.

"He had a couple of police officers who gave him good info that kept him two steps ahead of the FBI and DEA, but he didn't know his own people were snitching to the DEA and FBI." Curtbone said. The feds were cultivating informants by busting them, threatening them with mandatory sentences, flipping them and putting them back out on the street. The alphabet boys were all up in Rayful's B.I. They were arresting street level dealers and trying to turn members of Rayful's crew. Working their way up the hierarchy of Ray's organization and getting all the information and intelligence on the crew they could. The same tactics the feds used to topple Mafia empires they applied to Rayful's crew. Rayful and his people didn't stand a chance.

In the fall of 1988, Alta Rae Zanville started making moves. She accumulated a Porsche, several minks, a beautiful house and a Mercedes. She was getting comfortable in the life, and Rayful extended every courtesy to her. Bootsie tried to warn her to be careful. She told Zanville, "I think Rayful just gonna wait until this stuff cools off." But Zanville didn't think the investigation was monitoring her. She was wrong.

On December 19, she drove her white Porsche into the parking lot of Hogates, a restaurant on the city's Maine Avenue wharf in Southwest. She was wearing a squirrel coat and carrying 1.5 kilos of cocaine on the back seat.

As she emerged from her Porsche, FBI and DEA agents swooped in and busted her. She admitted to selling the kilos and became an informant.

No matter how much Rayful trusted her, she wasn't cut out for the life. She snitched him out at the first opportunity. For her cooperation, the government didn't seize any of her property and granted her full immunity. The DEA placed taps on her phone immediately. She was working for Uncle Sam.

Rayful called the next day. "I hear you been arrested," he said. She denied it and Rayful accepted what she said. It was the biggest mistake he ever made. Trusting Zanville would put the nails in Rayful's coffin and bury him also. For the next four months, Alta Rae wore a body wire gathering evidence to use against Rayful.

"Ray knew they was on his tail because people were talking," Curtbone said. "He knew they was on to him. The feds would be taking photos. He used to say 'When they come get me I'm going to the feds. I'm a fed nigga. I'm not a Lorton nigga.'" Ray's attitude was that he was high profile, a major and big time drug dealer. Not just another corner hustler.

In 1989, the heat started coming down. A number of people in his inner circle gave him up to save their own asses. "The heat was stepping up more," Curtbone said. "They were coming in abundance." With the time the feds were threatening, it didn't matter how much money Rayful was making. Dudes were getting busted and trading info on Ray to get off. They weren't trying to do 10 or 20 years for Rayful Edmond.

Zanville wore the body wire while lunching with Rayful's mother Bootsie, on March 4, 1989. The FBI tuned in as they chatted about their friends who'd been busted. Rayful's mother provided the final pieces of evidence that the feds needed in her conversation with Zanville, outlining Rayful's rise in the drug game.

"She was a mom to me. But also a personal friend," Rayful said. "My mom was my friend. She told all the things I told her to an informant." That taped conversation fucked Rayful up, but what could he do? It wasn't some snitch telling on him; it was his mom bragging about him being successful, to someone she trusted, that turned out to be a snitch.

During Rayful's reign, people died, people ate, people worked, people went to jail, and people became addicted to cocaine. Although Edmond's track record was one of praise for aspiring baby Nino Browns and wannabe head honchos, right is right and wrong is wrong. And Rayful was wrong. He just didn't know it.

As the law closed in on Edmond he watched his empire crumble. "When they did come get Ray he knew they was coming." The D.C. hustler says. "He was liquidating all his assets. I heard this out Ray's mouth, he said, 'I got eight million. They coming. I'm out.'" But with the conspiracy laws and the War on Drugs there was no out anymore.

During the investigation, one detective posed a question to an 11-year-old with knowledge of the network. "To be in Rayful's crew, would you kill somebody? Would you use a pump shotgun? The kid answered, 'I might. I could get my own bank.'" The detective related.

Young people were in awe of Rayful and routinely offered their services to him at nightclubs he frequented. "He'd say, 'Give me a call. I'll give you some work to do.'" The detective said. "If the youths were good, Edmond would promote them to more trusted positions and reward them with a car."

The investigation into Edmond's enterprise uncovered that Ray was paying the bills on 40 or so cars. These were cars he owned or had access to and cars that he bought for his family, friends and workers. It was something little to Rayful. He was the Big Willie, the HNIC. He could afford to be benevolent and reward his crew's loyalty.

He could pick the best and brightest D.C. had to offer because everybody wanted to be in Rayful's crew. With his charisma and charm he drew workers to him like Lil' Wayne attracts groupies. Everything came easy to him. Everybody wanted to be down with Ray. He was the superstar of the city.

At some point the network stopped keeping written records of the accounts because Rayful learned that police had found references to records in earlier raids. With no records, Rayful worried that members of his family would short change him. He tried to keep all the information in his head as he had when he was younger. But his operation had grown so big it was impossible. There was just too much information.

As the police investigation intensified, Rayful expanded the operation to different houses, apartments and hotel rooms around the metropolitan area. He used new locations as stash spots to count the money and package the cocaine. He enacted new policies to try and keep everything kosher. Rayful was strict with his workers, a code of conduct prohibited narcotics use. "It was run just like a major corporation." The detective said. "You had a chairman of the board and it went down from there." But despite his safeguarding measures the seizures started adding up. Rayful was taking huge losses.

During one search of an Arlington apartment belonging to Tony Lewis, police found clothing with $6,000 price tags and 70 pairs of shoes. "The cheapest pair was $600," the detective said. Tony Lewis and Rayful weren't cheap when it came to their wardrobe. These young brothers went all out, all the time.

Also uncovered were records of all expenses paid trips to the Super Bowl in San Diego on a chartered plane, limo bills for the Mike Tyson/Michael Spinks fight in Atlantic City and numerous $25000 pendants that identified crew members. The evidence was starting to become overwhelming. The money spent and accounted for was staggering.

The feds knew that Rayful's crew understood they were under surveillance and were attempting to hide their activities from law enforcement. Sometime in 1988, officer Jerome Sitck of the Metropolitan Police Department and two other officers were patrolling the area of 407 M Street, Northeast and they observed four individuals in a dark colored Mercedes Benz in front of the house. One of them exited the Mercedes and ran from the area. Another one, Johnny Monford, was detained for questioning. Inside the Mercedes, the officers recovered $9,000 in cash.

With all the busts Rayful was forced to take care of his crew by making sure they were always represented by a paid lawyer, an unusual sight in D.C. Superior Court for youths with no visible signs of employment. This was another added expense and drain on his resources. But in the Rayful Edmond crew everything was done first-class. The families of those killed in the line of duty received thousands of dollars in cash. Edmond and others showed up in t-shirts that said, *We'll Miss You* at the funerals. With everything crashing in around him, Rayful continued to try to do the right thing and continued to try and operate his business. But it was all for nothing. As the heat closed in Rayful said, "I am not the person the U.S. government is making me out to be."

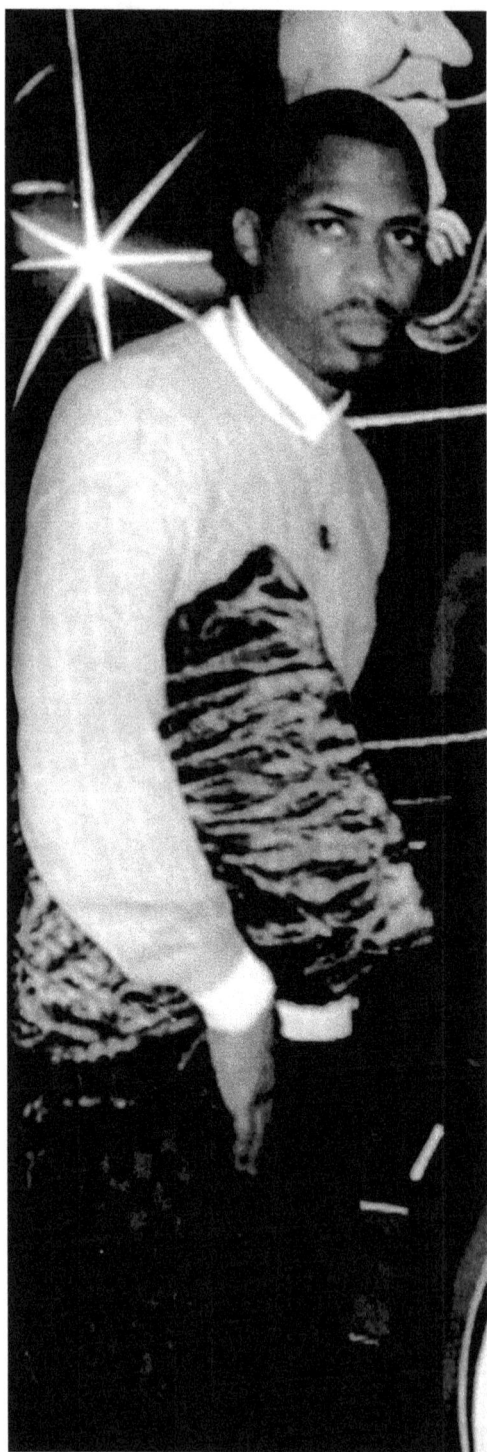

Rayful Edmond

Antonio ``Yo`` Jones

Tony Lewis

Part 7

Busted

"Rayful was balling, but he wasn't like they made him out to be." Mr. T says. "A lot of that was for the media and public. He was just the wrong nigga in the wrong place at the wrong time." For more than a decade the D.C. area was plagued by the crack epidemic. People were scared to walk out of their houses, and the man held responsible for the district's descent into crack cocaine hell was Rayful Edmond.

"Yeah, the media hype really helped with the conviction verdict. They made us look like some of the most notorious dudes on the planet. We knew that was a part of their plan though. I admit we were getting a nice piece of change back then, but not like they were reporting. The media's job is to make an average story interesting or more appealing than it actually was. I know they had a field day with us, because there were so many different people providing their input." Yo said.

The government was committed to convicting Rayful by any means necessary. The feds claimed that Ray turned the streets of D.C. into the biggest open air drug market ever seen. The coordination of local and federal drug and surveillance helped prosecutors build their case against Rayful. At the age of 24, Rayful's reign as the king of coke in Washington, D.C. was over.

April 15, 1989 was takedown day. A week before the scheduled arrests ABC news anchor Ted Koppel called lead prosecutor Betty Ann Soiefer. The network star was planning to televise a town meeting about Washington that would be called *Divided City* and he knew every detail about the Edmond raid. He wanted his camera crews to tape the operation. Soiefer turned him down, but Koppel said he would send his cameras anyway.

Two days before the raid, an informant told DEA agent Cornille that Tony Lewis had called Edmond with most of the raid details. Lewis even saw the arrest warrants. The warning allowed Edmond to liquidate some of his assets. Ray was turning as much capital from his organization into cash as he could. The leak was subsequently found to be a courthouse clerk familiar with Lewis. The Rayful Edmond crew was forewarned.

"I can't even remember who the fuck was on the other line. The only thing I heard was, 'they're coming, they're coming.' I wasn't a college graduate, but I knew who the fuck they were referring to." Yo said. When the feds come, they come with much fanfare and it's always a big affair when the alphabet boys are involved. "They got Ray on income tax weekend," Smoke says. "The government alerted the media as soon as he was taken into custody. Ray had slipped through so many times that they wanted to get as much publicity as they could."

The Rayful Edmond bust was front page news. *The Washington Post* and *Washington Times* ran headline after headlines. "I watched the news and saw all of my crew go down one by one," Yo said. "I was still trying to figure out the best way to get the money for my lawyer ready and trying to make sure my family was okay."

Edmond was arrested in the 900 block of Northeast at his girlfriend's apartment on Emerson Street. Edmond opened the door and officers aimed pistols at him while piling into the apartment. He was arrested in his boxer shorts. He was very nonchalant and casual about the event, like he had nothing to worry about.

"I heard that you were looking for me," Rayful said to the police. "Why didn't you call?" The cops cuffed Rayful, put him in the police car and they drove to DEA headquarters. "What do I have to do to get out tonight?" Rayful asked as if inquiring about the weather. "Can I call my lawyer?" Rayful thought the feds didn't have anything concrete on him. He was never caught with any drugs or money, so he figured he was good to go.

Rayful took his whole arrest very casual, like it wasn't serious. He didn't expect to be in jail for more than a couple of hours. At his arraignment he said nothing more than his name. When a U.S. Magistrate denied bond to him and 16 others swept up with him in the weekend arrests, Edmond was surprised. He figured it would be one night in jail at the most. "I didn't know how bad my situation was or how it was going to turn out." He said.

According to the affidavit unsealed in U.S. District Court, Edmond's group sold hundreds of kilograms of cocaine and crack over a five year period and "employed numerous people to obtain, package and distribute narcotics, launder profits and violently enforce the code of conduct within the organization." Eighteen people, most of who were connected to the organization, provided information about the group during the 18 month investigation carried out by the DEA, FBI and D.C. police.

According to the affidavit, the witnesses included drug and money couriers, buyers, street lieutenants, sellers, a member of the Crips, a security guard and a lifelong friend and associate of Edmond. When it came to telling, it took all types. The feds didn't discriminate. "We're all individual men, we didn't have one person calling the shots, but we came together as a family during times of crisis. You know every town or city has rats." Yo said. All the weak links in Ray's crew had been exposed. "This is the most significant law enforcement operation here directed at a cocaine distribution network," U.S. Attorney Jay Stephens said. "This is the principal case. Based on our intelligence, Edmond's group distributed up to 50 percent of the cocaine coming in. It was a close-knit family organization with enforcers, runners, lieutenants and money counters." More than 150 people jammed the hallways of the federal courthouse at Third Street and Constitution Avenue, Northwest waiting for the arraignment of Rayful Edmond. Some of the spectators were waiting outside the fourth floor courtroom hours before the proceedings began. Many in the crowd said they were relatives of the suspects. It turned into a major media event.

"The marshals told us we were like movie stars. All over TV." Curtbone said. *The Washington Post* was hyping up the case, running headlines such as, *Addicted to the Dollar, Flashy D.C. Drug Lord's Generosity Lured Large Pool of Employees, Police say.* Seven Assistant U.S. Attorneys were assigned to the case. The feds weren't taking any chances. They were using all their resources.

The affidavit said Edmond was aware of the impending operation in February and began selling and transferring his assets to avoid seizure. Still authorities seized four houses owned by Ray's relatives and 15 cars. Among the property seized by the feds included a Chevrolet Corvette, a Jaguar XJS convertible, a Mercedes-Benz 190E and residences at 1009 Peconic Place, Upper Marlboro, Maryland and 14518 London Lane, Bowie, Maryland. Assorted personal property was also seized from these houses. The feds were grabbing everything they could get their hands on.

"We've taken down a major distributor in the city. That sends a message to the community that we are serious, that we are going to close this drug distribution market down." D.C. Police Chief Maurice Turner said. "We don't see any major organized gangs in D.C. This group was a loosely organized, family unit." In the media and the hood, Rayful's arrest had the streets buzzing. His myth was slowly advancing into street lore.

In custody Rayful was getting the V.I.P. treatment from guards. He was treated like a godfather in jail. A revolving door of visitors came to pay their respects and to get his blessings to start up their own operations in his territories. Like Don Corleone in *The Godfather,* Rayful gave his approval to the upstarts.

"I was in the district jail in Washington, D.C. on lockdown awaiting trial on a drug conspiracy case, one of the biggest drug cases that ever came out of the city." Yo said. "Some of my co-defendants were Rayful Edmond, Tony Lewis, Jerry Millington, John Monford, Melvin Butler, Keith Cooper, just to name a few. We had one hell of a team. The Rayful Edmond Crew.

"The D.C. jail was a good place to do time, until they

moved us. The D.C. jail officials called the U.S. Marshal at the federal courthouse and asked that we be moved for security reasons. They said they no longer had control, because corrections officers would do anything to be in our good graces. The C/O's were very respectful and showed us mad love.

"One day they walked through our cell block with an official tour, looked in Rayful's cell and found an XL pizza box from Pizza Hut. Then they started looking everywhere and came up with an empty bottle of Remy Martin. We stayed twisted in that place. The very next day our asses were out of there, they sent some of us to the Marine base, down in Quantico, Virginia and the other half went to Fort Mead in Laurel, Maryland."

The arrests and subsequent trials were widely covered by local and national media. A circus atmosphere ensued that rivaled the fanfare of a presidential election. *NBC Dateline* aired a program on Rayful in 1989 calling him the *$300 Million Man,* before the trial. Rayful became the face of all that was wrong with the capital's inner-city drug frenzy. "It was so big, it was impossible for him to get a fair trial," Curtbone said. "They made Ray seem so powerful and so dangerous."

Approximately 50 news reports dealing in some way with Edmond or his co-defendants were published during the five months between Edmond's arrest and the beginning of his trial. The reports linked Edmond to Colombian drug cartels and as many as 30 homicides. The negative publicity pronounced a verdict of guilty to the world before he was even tried.

By Highway and Air, California Connection Supplied D.C., The Washington Post headline read. *Making a D.C. link to the Colombian Source* was another headline they ran. In the wake of such publicity and because the media had seized upon Edmond's name as a label for the case, there was no way Rayful could get a fair trial in D.C. Plus with the connections to the Colombian drug cartels, which were extremely newsworthy at the time, Rayful's crew seemed nefarious.

Numerous homicides were linked by law enforcement sources to gang members. The shooting deaths of two youths in a small Chinese carryout restaurant at 102 Rhode Island Avenue Northwest; the October 27, 1988 killing of a bystander outside the Chapter III nightclub in Southeast; and the deaths of Donald Ray and Darrell Birdine in the Sursum Corda housing development. One suspected key member of the alleged drug network, Darryl Murchison, was gunned down March 11 at Fifth and K Streets Northeast. The feds blamed Rayful for all these murders.

The affidavit also said a group member, Columbus Daniels, shot and killed Brandon Terrell at the direction of Edmond outside the Chapter III nightclub on June 23, 1988. The feds charged that Little Nut, purposely and deliberately with premeditated malice, killed Brandon Terrell with a pistol. The government said that Edmond sold Terrell drugs and that Terrell refused to pay for them. He also established his own drug ring to compete with Rayful's. A serious no-no in the inner-city drug trade and crack bonanza.

On the night of Terrell's death, he allegedly insulted Rayful and argued with him at Chapter III. Later outside the club, they argued again and Edmond withdrew, but upon his signal Little Nut, who was waiting with a pistol, shot and killed Terrell. The indictment alleged other murders, but this was the only count charged.

The document also stated that street sellers, lookouts and lieutenants originally were paid between $400 and $800 a week, but these salaries were increased to between $3,300 to $5,000 per week. Several of the lieutenants paid themselves the same amount. Walkie-talkies were used so the lieutenants, sellers and lookouts could communicate and ensure that the sellers would not be robbed.

The bags of cocaine were distributed to street sellers by lieutenants with names like Mad Dog, Whitey and Fat Cheese. After selling the crack, the sellers turned in their proceeds over to lieutenants, who then turned the money directly over to Edmond. The hierarchy of the organization was insulted at the top, so no drugs had to be handled, but with the conspiracy laws it didn't matter.

The group allegedly bought expensive cars- Mercedes Benz's, BMW's, Ford Broncos and Jaguars- often for cash. The Rayful Edmond organization, as it was called in the affidavit, operated mainly out of the M Street row house at 407 M Street, Northeast that served as a hub for the conspiracy. The house was owned by Edmond's grandmother, who was not charged. The group used several other houses and apartments in the District, Maryland and Virginia to distribute crack. They traveled back and forth from L.A. and transported cocaine by plane and van.

"It did shock me when people told on Ray. His mom killed him by bragging to someone that was wearing a wire. I couldn't believe she was talking like that." D.C. Chris says. Rayful's most trusted and closest confidants were the ones who did him in. Royal Brooks said at first he tried to protect Rayful, but he couldn't withstand the feds pressure.

"Ray trusted Royal with his life and it cost him his life. That was his quote unquote best friend," Curtbone said. "He was hurt that Royal and Zanville went against him." Alta Rae Zanville, his advisor and Royal Brooks, Ray's childhood friend proved to be the star witnesses against him. When the tide turned, it crashed in on Rayful, his family and crew.

On May 15, 1989, a grand jury handed down a 39 count indictment charging 29 persons with conspiracy to violate narcotics laws and various other offenses. The 44 count superseding indictment was filed on June 20, 1989 charging Edmond and all the defendants with a variety of narcotics related activities, weapon offenses, murder and other crimes of violence in regards to the operation of a large scale cocaine distribution conspiracy that existed from 1985 until Edmond's arrest.

The government said Edmond led a group of family members and friends who conspired to distribute large amounts of cocaine in the Northeast Washington neighborhood where many of them lived and where Edmond grew up. Those involved in the conspiracy were Edmond, Melvin "Mel Dogg" Butler, Tony Lewis, Edmond's half-brother Emmanual "Mangie" Sutton, his half-sister Bernice "Niecey" McGraw and her husband David McGraw, Edmond's cousin Johnny Monford, his aunt Armaretta Perry, Edmond's sister's boyfriend Jerry Millington, Antonio "Yo" Jones, Keith "Cheese" Cooper, Columbus "Little Nut" Daniels, Edmond's mother Constance "Bootsie" Perry, his sister Rachelle Edmond, Curtis "Curtbone" Chambers, Katrina Wade, Jeffrey Thompson who was married to Rayful's sister Raynice, Robert "Fila Rob" Hardy and Edmond's brother Melvin "Melbo" Stewart.

The Washington Post declared, *Sweep Broke Drug Ring, Officials say; 50% of Cocaine in D.C. Tied to Group.* Many of the family members supervised the retail side of the street operation counting the money, packaging and distributing the cocaine destined for the open air drug market at Orleans and Morton Place, Northeast. The strip was a goldmine for Rayful and his family, but now it was over.

Between 1986 and 1989, police observed steady trafficking in cocaine and crack on the strip, overseen by the defendants. In 1988, police obtained search warrants for several stash houses on the strip and carried out five separate searches, finding guns, money and significant amounts of drugs. With all the evidence the feds had compiled it didn't look good for the Rayful Edmond crew.

"Rayful Edmond is no hero. He is simply a thug with a wasted past and a hopeless future," the U.S. Attorney said as the trial began at the U.S. District Court building that occupied an entire city block on the North Side of Constitution Avenue where it intersected with Pennsylvania Avenue at Third Street. Constructed of buff colored limestone, it wasn't an unappealing structure and the small park to one side with the expansive courtyard in front, gave it an open, unimposing feeling.

The National Gallery's East Wing was directly across the street and the Capitol was just four blocks up the hill. It was a court for trying corrupt senators, judges, spies and federal officials. But in mid-September 1989 it was the venue to try Rayful Edmond. *Drama Looms Large at Edmond Drug Trial, The Washington Post* headline trumpeted.

On August 9th, the court filed an order severing the

defendants and counts into three separate groups. The first trial arising out of the superseding indictment, which involved 11 defendants, began on September 11, 1989. That trial, which put the street legend Rayful in the defendant's box, generated a great deal of media attention. There was a tremendous amount of scrutiny concerning every aspect of the trial.

"The first trial was a complete zoo. They had us in one of those courtrooms they normally would use for terrorists, bulletproof glass and everything. Their reasoning for that was so that we couldn't intimidate any jurors or witnesses I guess. They ultimately wanted to put up shields, so that no one could see us in the courtroom. They actually set up some monitors on the other side of the glass, but the U.S. Court of Appeals told them that they couldn't do that." Yo said.

The jury selection was extremely difficult. Many feared they would be killed if recognized. Before ordering juror anonymity in the case, the trial judge received from the government, an in camera submission describing threats to witnesses. This submission stated that two confidential sources had reported that Edmond's father intended to "take care of the witnesses" in the case, and that a caller falsely representing herself as a relative of Alta Rae Zaneville, had telephoned an assistant U.S. attorney in an effort to elicit information on her whereabouts.

"When Rayful got busted it was big news. I mean big news. It seemed he was the biggest drug dealer the world had ever seen." Da Kid from Southeast says. The gang was believed to have committed over 30 murders, including the attempted murder of a local pastor, the Reverend Bynum, who was shot 12 times during an anti-drug march in his Orleans Place neighborhood.

Judicial officials, fearful of reprisals from members of Edmond's gang, imposed unprecedented security during the trial. Juror's identities were kept secret before and during the trial and their seating was enclosed in bulletproof glass. Edmond was jailed at the maximum security facility at Marine Corps Base Quantico in Virginia and flown to the Federal Court House in Washington, D.C. by helicopter each day for his trial. Authorities took this unusual step due to heightened fears of an armed escape attempt.

"The military barracks was a totally different experience," Yo said. "In June of 89 we were sent to Quantico and put in the barracks with the military prisoners. They cleared out the hole there and put us in that tight-ass joint. We were in pre-trial and that's how they justified moving us with the help of the U.S. Military, the FBI, Federal Bureau of Prisons and the U.S. Marshal's office put together a high level of security strategy.

"We were still civilians, so the MPs there couldn't take custody of us. They sent some guards down from USP Lewisburg for about a month, then they changed guards. Some came from FCI Petersburg, Virginia. Throughout all of the moving, we still were going to court every day. Every morning the traffic moved slow coming up to D.C. and we started being late for court every day.

"So the Marshal's asked the military for their help once again. The next morning a Huey helicopter landed in the stockade's recreation yard. They put us in the helicopter and we flew to court every morning from that point. Being late became a big problem for the Marshal's office and the U.S. Military wanted to help by being a part of their big show. Every morning we flew over the dirty-ass

Potomac River.

"The helicopter flight plan called for them to only fly that route. Once we entered D.C.'s air space we flew to Anacostia Park, they had a landing pad for park service helicopters. The Marshal's put together one hell of a team that met us every morning.

"They had snipers on the rooftops and these muthafuckas had weapons I'd never seen before. Shit like MP5s, M16s with 100 round drums. A swat team was assigned to us but the feds ran the show to make us look like some of the most notorious brothers that ever came out of D.C.

"We all know that was just the media trying to hype the situation, because D.C. was and will always be home to all gangsters, both young and old. The U.S. Attorney at the time was J.B. Stevens. He had a real hard on for us. He had help from the area news media, both electronic and newspapers. They put on one hell of a show, with only one thing in mind. A guilty verdict." With everyone aligned against them the Rayful Edmond crew was doomed and were portrayed as evil personified.

"They made it seem like a bunch of animals from Africa," Curtbone said. "The trial was a circus, it was all premeditated on their part. It was a no win situation. Unknown jurors, bulletproof glass, Ray flying in from Quantico everyday by helicopter." Also Rayful's attorney of record, Art Reynolds, was named as an unindicted coconspirator and banned from representing him.

"The judge was racist." Smoke says. "His son died of crack. He wanted Ray and them to pay. Rayful was so powerful, the jurors had to sit behind bulletproof glass. The jury was anonymous. The judge told the assembled artists not to sketch the individual jurors accurately." The prosecution was using all the tools of the trade available to them to get Rayful convicted before the trial ever started.

"An anonymous jury protects the jury and protects the integrity of the trial." The prosecution said, but defense lawyers had a different opinion. "The only reason I can see to do it is to prejudice the jury. It's a tremendous tactical advantage for the prosecution. Instead of a presumption of innocence, there's a presumption of guilt." Edmond's lawyer argued. With so many co-defendants, the judge split them into three groups, three trials. The first with Rayful was a spectacle.

Twenty-nine people were originally indicted, but in August 1989 the district court severed the counts on the indictment alleging weapons offenses and crimes of violence from those alleging conspiracy and drug-related activity. The court further divided the defendants' indicted for drug crimes and conspiracy into two groups according to their roles in the enterprise, designating the leadership and principle members of the organization as Group I and the more peripheral actors as Group II.

The murder counts would be held in a third trial. Three separate trials were held. The Group I defendants were tried in late 1989. Other than the nine defendants who pled guilty, all of the defendants went to trial. Five other defendants, three of whom cooperated with the government, were also charged in the conspiracy, although they were not indicted.

At his 56 day trial Edmond never testified. He was separated from the spectators by bulletproof glass. He had nothing to say about the fact that one prospective witness was shot before trial and that the home of another witness was firebombed the night before she was to testify.

"The majority of the non-law enforcement witnesses I came in contact with during this period expressed great fear and anxiety about testifying publicly in this trial." Assistant U.S. Attorney Robert Andary said. "The witnesses were concerned about retaliation against themselves or their families because of their testimony, and assisting them to cope with this fear was a constant part of preparing and presenting the evidence in this case."

Ray sat quietly as his best friend, Royal Brooks, testified that he stored as much as 90 kilograms of cocaine and carried as much as $3 million of Edmond's money to arrange drug buys in L.A. He told the court that he regularly collected cocaine from Butler and others at various hotels and residences in the Washington area. His testimony was paramount to the prosecution. He was literally the straw that broke the camel's back.

"I actually came face to face with this hot muthafucka in 1991 when I was coming back to D.C. for court. Back in the day everyone came through FCI El-Reno, Oklahoma before getting shipped to their destination. I had no idea this clown was on the same plane with me until the inmates started to depart the plane. As people were walking by me I noticed this guy, wearing a blue D.C. jail jumpsuit, run over to the U.S. Marshal saying that he couldn't get off the plane right now because Antonio "Yo" Jones is back there.

"I didn't know what the fuck was going on until I saw the U.S. Marshal's officer bring his punk-ass pass me. I caught up with him again inside of the FCI. This time was on better terms, because one of the Marshals had already taken my cuffs and shackles off and wasn't paying attention to me. I slipped into the hallway where Royal was walking with four officers and caught him with a nice two piece before the officers could restrain me. His bitch-ass started hollering please keep him away from me. The feds gave me a few lumps for that shit, but it was well worth it."

Alta Rae Zanville acknowledged wearing a hidden microphone to collect evidence for the government. She testified that in 1988 in Tony Lewis' apartment, Robert "Fila Rob" Hardy and Rayful Edmond helped her load her suitcase with close to $2 million, which she later brought to California as payment for a shipment of cocaine.

James Minor gave detailed testimony about his delivery of cocaine to Robert "Fila Rob" Hardy on numerous occasions and numerous recorded conversations between Rachelle Edmond and Alta Rae Zanville, exposing the conspiracy and all those involved, were played for the court. With the insurmountable evidence, the conspiracy laws and all the snitches, it seemed like a slam dunk for the government.

Alonzo Mourning, the Georgetown Hoya and future NBA player was called to testify at the trial for the defense. A stand up move on his part. Mourning testified that he made several visits to the home of Edmond and up to 10 visits to the home of Jerry Millington. But he said he had not seen any drugs, large amounts of cash or drug paraphernalia at either home.

In visits to Millington's home in the fall of 1988 and early 1989, Mourning said, he and John Turner, a former Georgetown teammate who introduced Mourning to Edmond, watched sports events on television. Mourning said he stopped associating with Edmond after John

Thompson, the Georgetown coach, warned the team against it earlier that year. When it counted though, Mourning kept it real.

Rayful remained quiet, even as his two lawyers screamed and argued with each other. He never testified before the jury, which for security reasons was the first anonymous jury in D.C. history. At one point however, he did pass a note to a young woman working for a TV station that said he thought she was cute. Ever the charmer, Rayful worked his magic, but the court and judge were charm proof. Rayful's legendary charisma meant nothing to them.

"Everybody had incentives to lie. Royal said a lot of things about me. Me and him was like brothers, I couldn't believe him coming to court saying things like that about me." Rayful said. He was upset his friend testified against him, but he should have seen that dude wasn't cut like that. As the trial entered its third week it took another unexpected twist.

The U.S. District Court Judge, Charles Richy, excluded the public from the trial, leaving the media to act as its surrogate. The judge's order was only the last in an almost daily series of outbursts and unexpected events, which often overshadowed the courtroom testimony. Like a three ring circus, there was always multiple acts going on.

At the center of it was the tense pas de deux between Judge Richy and William Murphy, a former judge who was one of Edmond's attorneys. At one point during the trial the judge reminded Murphy that there was only one judge in the courtroom, not two. Murphy bristled at the judge, clearly showing his distaste for the reminder.

The unpredictable atmosphere prompted discussion

among defense attorneys and prosecutors about the possibilities of a mistrial. It also touched off debate about the ability of the government to prosecute complex, multi-defendant drug investigations, in which a cloud of fear hung over the proceedings, affecting both jurors and witnesses alike. For our nation's capital this was a trial with Mafia-like implications that they clearly weren't used to. The political and public relations ramifications were a nightmare.

With allegations of witness harassment, death threats, prosecutorial misconduct, and judicial bias, the trial was turning into a carnival of epic proportions. Barnum and Bailey weren't in town, but it didn't stop the greatest show on earth. The clowns were in effect with the feds playing the starring role.

It was human tragedy at its best. Prosecutors demanded investigations of leaks to the media, while defense attorneys argued for drug urinalysis tests for prosecution witnesses. The judge had a hard job maintaining control. He acted as the ringmaster, directing the various acts and melodramas, but the chaos prevailed.

At one point, a shoving match appeared imminent between prosecutor Betty Ann Soiefer and Murphy, who likened the prosecutor to football player William "The Refrigerator" Perry. An exchange between Murphy and Soiefer over the insinuation erupted into a shouting match. When Soiefer tried to prevent him from returning to the lectern, Murphy told Soiefer to sit down.

"You are not going to tell anyone to sit down," snapped Richy, reminding Murphy that he was the judge. "And Ms. Soiefer is judge number two," Murphy shot back. Later Murphy complained to the judge that if he tried to "push" Soiefer aside he "probably would be in handcuffs and on my way to Leavenworth." The theatrics aside, the trial was quickly turning into a reality TV-type event.

"Let the record reflect I fear when Ms. Soiefer approaches me from behind," Murphy told the judge after the incident in which Soiefer physically attempted to block him from using the lectern. It was apparent from the beginning that the team of three prosecutors, Soiefer, Robert Andary and Barry Tapp had made their minds up and set their sights on Edmond and his crew.

They were on a mission to bury them under the jail. As the soap opera continued the drama loomed large. Many of the histrionics were recounted on nightly television news shows, as defense attorneys addressed cameras on the courthouse steps, in what became a daily sideshow to the courtroom proceedings.

Over 160 witnesses were scheduled to be called, but one key witness, Deborah Phillips, decided not to testify because prosecutors mistakenly mailed a letter outlining her cooperation agreement to her home where she lived with her boyfriend, one of the defendants. A major prosecution blunder. But they pushed on diligently, staying the course and calling their witnesses one by one. Throughout the testimony, the 12 defense attorneys argued vigorously for a mistrial. Anything to help their clients. What Edmond's attorney started, the others joined in on.

"Murphy is creating the atmospherics that could provoke a mistrial," an observer said. "He is constantly picking away at everything. Some might see it as annoying, but eventually he is going to hit on something." Media members packed the courtroom, watching the story unfold. It was like MTV's *The Real World* in a way. The drama and tension were thick.

Edmond's attorneys had attempted to cast the spotlight on his father, Big Ray, described as a "high rolling gambler" by two witnesses. The defense contended that Edmond, known for his lavish lifestyle, received money from his father. Law enforcement sources told *The Washington Times* that the elder Edmond was the subject of a Justice Department probe by an organized crime strike team. It was that investigation that led investigators to begin their probe of Rayful Edmond.

The jurors were sequestered and known only by number to the judge, prosecutor and defense. "The potential consequences of somebody in the audience from the general public recognizing one of the jurors or vice versa are simply too serious," the judge said. "And the remedies available to the court, such as perhaps having to declare a mistrial, are too extreme."

According to the government evidence, the conspiracy involved a multi-layered operation, its focus on a two block area of Morton Place and Orleans Place, known as the strip, which Edmond ran and maintained from 1986 through 1989. In operating the drug business, sellers, paid by the day or week, worked in eight hour shifts, supplying product for the customers. They clocked in like they were working in a factory.

Demand for drugs along the strip was so intense during that period that sellers sometimes sold out their supplies within minutes. Individuals dubbed lieutenants of the organization including Cooper and Sutton, supplied dealers including juveniles, with bundles of cocaine, collecting money from them and shouting warnings when police entered the area.

These lieutenants, along with Millington, Yo and Monford supervised the strip, controlling the supply of cocaine and overseeing sellers. To supply the strip, several family members of Edmond, including David and Bernice McGraw and Armaretta Perry, packaged cocaine at various sites. They ran an assembly line like packaging production.

Once packaged, the cocaine was stored at various houses and apartments of the co-conspirators. Edmond lieutenants such as Dave McGraw and James Minor took delivery of these drugs and distributed them to safe houses on the strip and Bates Street, which was the operation Tony Lewis ran. The crew had very defined roles and responsibilities.

The government presented wiretap conversations in which Edmond and Lewis discussed their arrangements to retrieve drugs from California couriers and the current inventory and location of their drugs, and Edmond directed Lewis, to whom he would provide drugs for retail distribution. These conversations between Edmond and Lewis showed that Lewis worked under Edmond's direction. There was also evidence of the significant overlap between the strip and the Bates Street enterprise.

James Minor and Dave McGraw, who handled deliveries, were deeply involved in operations at both the strip and Bates Street. Testimony by police officers and co-conspirators demonstrated that Yo and Millington served as enforcers, whose role was to protect those involved in street level sales on the strip and that they engaged in acts of violence under the direction of Rayful to protect the territory, profits and operations of the organization. The witnesses testimony painted a picture of an efficiently run business with regular paydays and work shifts with Sundays off.

The government also presented evidence that the

Edmond organization acted as a drug wholesaler. The prosecutors essentially split the trial into two segments: retail and wholesale. The government presented evidence that Edmond associates Royal Brooks, Alta Rae Zanville, Tony Lewis and Edmond himself made trips to L.A. in the late-80s to arrange for and pay for shipments of cocaine to Washington. Tony Lewis and Edmond pooled their money to finance million dollar multi-kilogram cocaine purchases from their L.A. connections.

James Minor testified that "he and David McGraw picked up fifty kilograms of cocaine from a gentleman from California at the Day's Inn Hotel in Crystal City, Virginia in August, 1988." In the city Tony Lewis and Edmond were seen as partners, although Edmond was the more public of the two, as Lewis preferred to remain behind the scenes. The two youthful drug lords also formed a syndicate in D.C. with other major dealers, in an effort to quell the violence bloodying the drug markets.

"When he started out, it was just like, you know, like he was doing hand to hand, him and Johnny on the corner selling and they was getting it from Big Ray and then he, it just got too big, he just up and went out on his own." Bootsie Perry said to Alta Rae Zanville while being secretly recorded. These were the words that sealed Rayful's fate.

"That's not something I said, ladies and gentlemen, but his mother." The prosecutor told the jury after playing them the incriminating tape. Alta Rae Zanville, and the tapes she made while wearing a body wire, were the star attractions of the trial. The incriminating comments from Rayful's mother, caught on tape, were a godsend for the prosecution.

"They were actually executing slim without the death penalty," the D.C. gangster says. "He had Mayor Barry at his trial along with others. That's when he had respect. When he was in the ring with Rome clutching." A gentleman gangster, Rayful Edmond fought the good fight.

One hundred and sixty witnesses and 800 pieces of evidence, including tapes filled with coded discussions, in sometimes undecipherable Pig Latin, were presented in the 56 day trial presided over by U.S. District Court Judge Charles Richy. On one tape Edmond's cousin, repeatedly using words whose first letters spelled FBI, tried to warn his aunt, Armaretta Perry, that the agency might be bugging them.

"There was the general feeling that because of the bulletproof glass, the anonymous jury system, the number of Marshal's ringing the courtroom, the way in which the jury was selected and because of the general hype about the case and the amount of pretrial publicity, that all created a climate Rayful felt was going to make it difficult to get a fair trial," Edmond's lawyer said.

The most damaging evidence was the testimony of Alta Rae Zanville and Royal Brooks, who both testified in excruciating detail how they stored hundreds of pounds of cocaine and millions of dollars of cash for Edmond. Rayful was devastated that his two closet confidants turned on him. In fact, he seemed to be in shock as he watched them testify and detail his criminal activities. Zanville testified that she was asked to bring about $3 million in cash to L.A. on one occasion. She also gave the finite specifics on how Rayful did business and who played what part in the organization. Her testimony was extremely damaging to Rayful in particular.

She was even paid $12,000 by the government and when the trial was over, they also paid her relocation expenses and gave her a new identity. Meanwhile, Edmond's other traitor friend, Royal, a black male, didn't get a sweetheart deal like the white Zanville. He was taken into custody and served a reduced sentence in the BOP's Witsec program.

The prosecutors showed how Rayful spent money freely and had no explanation from where it came from. A parade of witnesses recounted a glittery lifestyle including a Jaguar convertible with gold-inlaid hubcaps, chauffeured limousines and $45,000 Rolex watches. Agents described finding 12 grand in dollar bills strewn like trash on the floor of Tony Lewis's Arlington apartment along with a jacket with a $3,500 price tag still attached. The three month trial dominated headlines and newscasts and was the first to be carried out under extraordinary security measures with more than 15 U.S. Marshal's in the courtroom. None of the defendants took the stand in their own defense and six witnesses linked Edmond directly to drug transactions. There was no way out for the Rayful Edmond Crew.

"I felt railroaded." Rayful said. "I honestly think I was. Everybody in D.C. knew about the case. I said to myself the jurors were not going to have any choice but to find you guilty." It was a harrowing reality Rayful and his crew had to face. The prospect of life in prison awaited them. During the trial, which produced 20,000 pages of transcripts, there were numerous incidents which justified the extra security measures. One of the defendants, Johnny Monford, made hand motions like he was loading a gun and pointed it in the direction of the judge and simulated firing the weapon twice. These actions were reported on the nightly news. Another incident occurred when government witness James Mathis was leaving the stand at the end of his testimony and Melvin Butler said, "I'm going to fuck you up."

As the trial went on Edmond got angry at his lawyers. At the urging of his father, he hired Baltimore attorney William Murphy to represent him, then later at the suggestion of his grandmother he hired James Robertson, a flamboyant Howard University law professor. Murphy and Robertson argued over courtroom strategy and at times even battled over who should speak to the judge. They tried to get Edmond to make a choice between them, but he refused.

"I didn't want nobody to say, 'Well, why did you let him down, make the other one feel uncomfortable?'" Rayful said. Edmond was also mad at the lawyers for his co-defendants. He thought the lawyers encouraged his friends and family to talk to the prosecution and blame everything on him. "I ain't trust none of their lawyers. They was sneaky. Looking out for their client's best interest. At one point it was like a family thing. I thought everyone was going to stick together. I look at any lawyer like an outside person. You haven't known him for a long time and you're going to let him turn you against one of your friends. You can't let them do that. I'm not into hurting none of my friends." Rayful said. But that would change in the future too.

"Now ladies and gentleman, obviously as you have heard, this is, indeed, a sad occasion when you have a history of a family that were nourished from the womb and has been dealing in narcotics in Washington D.C. on a scale larger than anything that we have heard about in the history of this particular city." The prosecutor said in his closing statement. "The scale of this narcotic trafficking which made millions of dollars is of an overwhelming magnitude." With the hype the case generated the results were a give-in. The trial was ugly, but the verdicts would be even uglier for Rayful and his crew.

On December 6, 1989, after the three month long trial, a jury of two men and 10 women announced their verdict on all defendants shortly after 10 a.m. After five days of deliberations, in what was the costliest trial ever held in the district, they were ready to enter a judgment. U.S. District Judge Charles Richy ordered the defendants and their attorneys to stand and face the jury before he read the verdicts. Edmond, dressed in a green turtleneck sweater and black dress shoes, faced the jury and briefly closed his eyes as the judge read the unanimous guilty verdict. Edmond was convicted of running a continual criminal enterprise, a count that called for life without parole and he still faced charged and uncharged murder counts. His future was looking very bleak indeed.

He appeared stunned at hearing his conviction on the charge. Judge Richy continued reading the verdicts for all the other defendants, including Rayful's aunt and sister, who also got jail time. His aunt, Armaretta Perry appeared to be consoling her son, co-defendant Johnny Monford, who was visibly upset by the verdicts. Other defendants stood silently or leaned toward their attorneys to talk in whispers. It took the judge more than 20 minutes to read the verdicts.

Tony Lewis, who was Edmond's partner, was convicted of conspiracy and interstate travel in aid of racketeering. Melvin Butler was convicted of conspiracy and illegal use of a telephone. Mangie Sutton, dubbed "director of street sales" was convicted of conspiracy and employing minors to sell drugs. Millington, the "vice president of street sales" was convicted of conspiracy. Antonio "Yo" Jones, "the vice president of enforcement" was convicted of conspiracy.

Edmond's sister Bernice McGraw, her husband David, Edmond's aunt Armaretta, his cousin Johnny and Keith Cooper were all convicted of conspiracy and for managing the retail operation out of Edmonds grandmother's house, which the feds dubbed "corporate headquarters." For the Rayful Edmond crew it truly was a family affair. Before dismissing those just convicted Judge Richy told them, "I wish each of you good luck and godspeed and I hope you can get on with your lives."

Of the 44 charges lodged against the defendants, the jury acquitted only one defendant on one count. "We were on trial for three months and they came back in four days. Some people have trial for a week and the jury is out two or three weeks." Rayful said. "I think me and my family and my friends all should have been found not guilty."

But the jury felt otherwise and Ray, his family and crew went down in flames, closing the chapter on one of D.C.'s biggest street legends, at least that was the prevailing thought at the time. "Yeah, they convicted a number of Ray's family members. Most notable was his mother, aunt, brothers, sisters and cousin. His cousin (Johnny Monford) went to Leavenworth with me. I was really proud of the way he stood tall in the penitentiary. He didn't take no shit from anyone. I taught him well. The feds are very vindictive; they love those cheese eating muthafuckas. They hated the majority of our mob, because we wasn't gonna tell them shit about anybody or anything." Yo said. The crew held true to the street code and stood strong in the face of adversity.

"I was found guilty by a so called jury of my peers." Yo said. "People I have never met, so I'm positive they were not my peers. None of them had the look in their eyes that showed they would do whatever it took to survive in a self-imposed war zone that I have embraced since my childhood."

U.S. Attorney Jay Stephens hailed the convictions as a victory "for all the people of the District of Colombia," and a warning to other drug dealers that law enforcement officials "stand shoulder to shoulder with the people of this community to turn the tide of drugs that have so devastated this city." Flanked by the three prosecutors who tried the case, Stephens said the verdict affirmed, "The ability of the criminal justice system to bring justice to those who seek to bring bloodshed and violence to our cities."

Edmond Convicted on All Counts in Drug Conspiracy Case; 10 Others Also Guilty, The Washington Post headline read. The convictions capped a massive two year investigation by the DEA, FBI and D.C. police, which pursued Edmond as his operation grew from its base in a quiet residential neighborhood in Northeast Washington to complete and utter domination over the whole city's drug market.

Edmond's rise and fall became milestones in the city's drug trade, a market previously dominated by small-time dealers in constant search of supplies. Edmond became the boss of bosses in the close quartered small city, which exists as our nation's capital. He was the Don Dada and a John Gotti-type figure to the inhabitants of the city.

Edmond's exploits were legendary among the city's youth, who knew stories about his gang's drug dealing and penchant for violence, investigators said. Edmond, who smiled through much of the trial, appeared shocked when the verdicts were read. "For those young people who have seen Mr. Edmond in his smiling ways over the years, they should have seen his crying ways in jail this morning," DEA Agent John Wilder mocked.

Edmond hugged James Robertson, one of his lawyers after the convictions were handed down. Robertson later said he experienced a feeling of "total helplessness as I sat next to my client." He called the convictions "absolutely devastating," but declined to say whether Edmond was innocent. "I am not in a position to say." Robertson said.

Outside the courtroom he told reporters, "I never thought this jury would convict him of the CCE count." Asked what Rayful said to him as the verdicts were read, Robertson replied, "He was just saying, 'It looks like we never really had a chance.'"

Edmond's other attorney, William Murphy- whose flamboyant courtroom style often set the judge on edge- said he planned to appeal the convictions. "We've lost this battle, but as General MacArthur said, 'We shall return.'" He called the district "the worst place at the worst possible time" for a drug trial, because of the city's anti-drug climate. With the devastation from the crack epidemic Rayful couldn't get a fair trial.

Murphy had sought a change of venue out of Washington because of pretrial publicity, but also as an alternative to some of the extensive security measures that marked the trial, including the anonymous jury, the U.S. Marshal's ringing the courtroom and spectators being kept behind bulletproof glass.

"They gave the impression these people were already considered guilty. Anybody with common sense to be on a jury can tell they're not being protected from the government, they're not being protected from the defense lawyers, they're being protected from the defense lawyers' clients. I mean, give me a break." He said.

Murphy was not surprised by the verdict, citing the extraordinary security measures during the trial. "I think he has an excellent chance on appeal." He said. Rayful and his crew tried to keep their heads up, but it was hard with the strong conviction against them. Hours after the verdict was reached, U.S. Attorney Stephens called the "sweeping guilty verdict" a victory for "those who live here, work here and visit here." He predicted the prospect of Edmond spending the rest of his life behind bars will "send a message that drug dealing is not a victimless crime." Appearing at a news conference with representatives of the DEA, FBI and U.S. Marshal's Service, who assisted in the investigation and the trial, Mr. Stephens said the verdict "leaves no doubt that justice can be a clarion call to all the people of this community to stand up and make it clear that we will not tolerate drug abuse in our streets."

On display before him was $3 million worth of drugs, more than a dozen weapons, $50,000 in $10, $20, $50 and $100 bills, plus jewelry the government seized from the Edmond drug organization and presented as evidence during the trial. All the accruements of the drug trade were on exhibit for everyone to see. The fanfare was incredible as the feds buried the Rayful Edmond crew. Metropolitan Police Chief Isaac Fulwood, responding to allegations that surfaced during the trial that police told members of the Edmond organization they were under investigation said during the news conference, "If there are D.C. police involved in this activity, they will be locked up." He declined to comment on whether the department was launching an internal investigation. "There were some allegations that have been looked at and are being looked at," added Douglas Gow, a special agent with the FBI. The verdict ensured that those who looked up to Edmond, one of the most powerful drug dealers in the city's history, and admired his flashy lifestyle "will see through jail bars a pathetic purveyor of human destruction," U.S. Attorney Stephens said. The victorious prosecuting office hailed the verdict as another battle won in the War on Drugs. Edmond's fall was a major victory for the soldiers fighting the drug war.

The media trumpeted the conviction of Edmond as a moral victory over the ills of society. The crack epidemic and the drug dealer's scourge were what society was fighting against. The battle against the Rayful Edmond crew was won.

Rayful felt cheated, but it didn't matter how he felt. Edmond attributed his conviction to the jury's perception of his extravagant spending habits. He felt they had no idea of what was really going on.

"They took that in the wrong way," he said. "They probably said to themselves, 'I've been working all my life. I have kids. I don't have this. How did he get all this?'" In Rayful's view the jury couldn't account for his lavish lifestyles so they convicted him accordingly and in spite of the lack of physical evidence linking him to drugs.

The jury according to Rayful was a group of "small-time" people, who had never been to Las Vegas or championship fights or driven expensive cars. Edmond believed the jury looked at him as a young black man and said, "How in the hell could he do all of this? And some of them mighta been 40 or 50-years-old and they never did nothing in their life."

Edmond also said he believed he would have received a fairer trial if the jury had been racially integrated. The twelve jurors were all black. In retrospect Rayful wanted white jurors, the opposite claim of what most black males request or want.

"I'm not racist," Edmond said. "But white people would have taken their time. They would have gone by the law. This jury never asked any questions about the law. Even me, I'm intelligent and I studied the legal issues. I don't understand some of it. I'm not saying they weren't intelligent. They just wasn't fair. They came in too quick. They didn't go over all the evidence or each charge."

Rayful had guessed the verdict, because of the questions the jury was asking the judge during the four days of deliberations. "If you look back, our jury was dumb," he said. "That was the thing that hurt us from the jump. They was dumb. Like they had to tell us where they went to school, what they do and most of them didn't even graduate.

"Half the jury didn't make it out of Junior High School. When you got somebody sitting up there, dumb, probably can't even write their name and they are judging your life- that's rough." Edmond believed the jury didn't understand what he was charged with.

"Even if I know somebody that's got drugs," he said. "And I say, 'Go get that for me' or something like that, well that don't make me guilty for what I'm charged with. Like one girl testified that I gave her a bag one day. Told her to take it somewhere. She never looked in it. I never told her what was in it.

"She did it, I gave her $300. She never looked in it or nothing. It could have been anything, so how can the jury misinterpret and say 'Okay, it must have been drugs?' You can easily be guilty of something, but that doesn't mean you have to get found guilty of it. Understand what I'm saying?"

Edmond said he was most shocked by the convictions of Tony Lewis, Antonio "Yo" Jones, Johnny Monford and Bernice McGraw. "I definitely thought they were going home," he said. Edmond said he felt badly for his family and friends and in particular for his mother who was convicted in a separate trial. "She's taking it hard. I'm her little baby. She feels it's her fault." Rayful said.

As for his mother's words on the Zanville tape, which were used to great effect by the prosecution to prove that he was a big drug dealer, Edmond said, "That's my mother and I gotta accept whatever comes from her. Eventually, you know, it hurt a lot of people by her saying that, so my being upset about it ain't going to help."

Edmond and his mother ran into each other at the D.C. jail, when they happened to be in the interview room at the same time to see their lawyers. "I told her she didn't have to explain nothing to me. That was all." He said. Whatever the circumstances Rayful was a mama's boy to the end.

Edmond said he could have helped himself by talking about what some of his friends were doing. "I'm taking a lot of weight for a lot of different people. What somebody else done is their business. I wasn't with them when they done it. I didn't encourage them to do it. I didn't know anything about it. There was no evidence that I personally sold drugs to anyone." He said.

He felt betrayed by many of the people he thought were his genuine friends. Several of them- Zanville and Brooks- testified against him. When it all came crashing down, people he thought would side with him sided with the feds. It was hard for Rayful to deal with.

"If they really cared and loved me like they was supposed to, they wouldn't have done certain things. They saying that they did this or did that for me. They didn't do it for Rayful. I didn't put no gun to their head. How can you say something bad about me, knowing you might have done something wrong yourself. People just saying things to help themselves. Everybody had incentives to lie. If they come to you and say you gonna go to jail if you don't tell us a certain thing." Rayful said.

Rayful was particularly mad at Brooks, his childhood friend. One of Edmond's lawyers called Brooks a "slippery witness" and scorned Brooks for agreeing to testify despite "his love for Rayful Edmond." In exchange for his testimony Brooks did very little jail time. He was a rat of the highest order.

"What he did, he can't ever go live in Washington D.C. and be safe," Rayful said. "I don't have to do nothing to him. It's just people in general." But Rayful's threats were never enacted and in the end proved groundless.

Looking back on the trial, Rayful wished he had taken the stand. "My lawyer was like, 'No, don't do that.' When your life is on the line, you got to do what you want to do. Your lawyer ain't gonna do the time." But Rayful learned this lesson too late. With the prosecution's victory, they moved onto the next trial.

The second trial, which involved nine defendants,

including Rayful's mother, began on February 26, 1990 and a jury returned guilty verdicts for all of the defendants on all counts on March 30, 1990. The defendants in the second trial were Willie Childress, Columbus Daniels, Rachelle Edmond, Robert Hardy, Ronald Morgan, Constance Perry, Melvin Stewart, Jeffrey Thompson and Raynice Thompson. The jury found each of these defendants guilty of participating in a conspiracy to violate the narcotics laws of the United States.

The trial on weapons and murder charges – the third trial- took place in June 1990. Rayful was on trial again with Columbus Daniels and others, the most significant charge being the Terrell Brandon murder. The feds weren't taking any chances with Edmond, they were trying to convict him of everything they could, so that he would never get out of jail.

"One of the subsequent trials didn't last long at all. They brought up a double homicide case I beat back in 88. Their goal was to tie me into the conspiracy as one of the main enforcers. They also brought up a body that Lil' Nut was convicted of previously. There was a third trial, but I had no knowledge of what took place. I was in Leavenworth doing my bid." Yo said.

With all the hoopla, Rayful Edmond was the hot topic in every social stratosphere. From the ghettos of the poverty stricken district to the upper middleclass suburbs of affluent Northern Virginia the Rayful Edmond story was front page news. *The Washington Post* had come out with a series of stories on Edmond, including, *The Mind of Rayful Edmond* and *Rayful Edmond: A Mystery Worth Solving*.

"It was the summer that the Rayful Edmond trial was going on," one city official said. "We realized that the youth of the city knew more about Rayful Edmond than great Civil Rights leaders who are really doing tremendous things and changing the world."

At the third trial, Rayful was convicted again. There were complications though. At least one witness, Robert Stewart, Ray's half-brother, refused to testify against Columbus Daniels at his first degree murder trial, as a result of a telephone call he received from Little Nut after he got the government's list of prospective witnesses. The climate of fear for the witnesses was high.

Another government witness, Theodore Smith, was approached in the D.C. jail by a prisoner who showed him two letters- one from Yo and one from a girl Valarea that asked him to tell Smith not to testify at Little Nut's trial. The letter from Yo was read in open court and it said, "These hot muthafuckas can't stop a good man from doing what he got to do. That fat muthafucka in 61-Cell, his name keep coming up in Little Nut's case, saying he was down the go-go the night dude got killed. Let everyone know about that hot fat bitch."

On September 17, 1990, the district court finally sentenced the crew. On Rayful, a sentence of mandatory life without parole was imposed. *Kingpin Faces Life for Drug Dealing, The Washington Times* headline read. His co-defendants that went to trial with him received similar sentences- Tony Lewis life, Little Nut life, Jerry Millington life, Yo life, Johnny Monford 405 months, Armaretta Perry 405 months, Melvin Butler 405 months, Mangie Sutton 320 months, Keith Cooper 320 months, David McGraw 292 months, Bernice McGraw 235 months and Rayful's mother, Bootsie Perry got 14 years.

As Rayful and his co-defendants went to do hard time, Alta Rae Zanville and Royal Brooks walked into a life in the federal witness protection program. They would be getting new names and new starts in life, while Rayful and his crew awaited a cell in the penitentiary. "If Ray and them didn't have all those murders, they wouldn't have got all that time." The D.C. hustler says. "That shit affected everyone, Tony Lewis, his mom, everyone."

Part 8

In Prison

"Through history, all the bad things happened to the good guys," Rayful said. "So I'm a good guy and just something bad happened to me and I'll overcome it sooner or later." But Rayful was in prison staring multiple life sentences in the face. His prospects were bleak, but he tried to make the best of a bad situation. "I will be home one day soon in a couple of years after my appeal," Rayful said. "We will all be home in a couple of years. I'm not a violent person. You can ask 1,000 people. In high school I was only in two or three fights. I was tried for murdering one of my best friends. Ask his family. They got to see that I ain't no murderer or nothing. Maybe I was a drug dealer, but I'm not all that bad of a person."

Exactly who and what Rayful was caused a lot of disputes in the Chocolate City. One woman, quoted anonymously in *The Washington Post* said she was pleased by the conviction because Edmond was responsible for "a whole lot" of bad things that happened to children with drugs. But a man recalled that Edmond gave his family money for flowers when a brother died and occasionally gave extra money for medicine and bus fare. "He may have been guilty of knowing the wrong people," the man said. "But Rayful wasn't no dope pusher." The director of a recreation center said the neighborhood children would miss Edmond. "They looked up to him. They respected him. If they ever had any problems, they could come and talk to him. They saw him as a big brother." He said.

Despite his life sentence without parole, Edmond was making plans for when he got out. He dreamed of opening a nightclub. In one room he would have big movie screens. In another room there would be pool tables. And in a special room, people could watch "like nasty movies." There would be a room for dancing and "a bar where they could buy all they want or whatever they want." There would be a dress code, "casual shoes, slacks and a jacket." Rayful knew it would be a success. "I could just put my name up there and people just come because they say 'Oh, that's Rayful's club.'" Rayful was a little delusional to say the least.

Edmond's long term home was a small cell at U.S.P. Marion. He described U.S.P. Marion as a place where prisoners wanted to take their frustrations out on each other. "I wish I was in another institution," Rayful said. He explained that U.S.P. Marion was for the most dangerous criminals and that he wasn't violent.

"I wouldn't wish this place on anybody." He said. When he wanted to hear the sound of another voice he had to call out carefully in a low voice, because he didn't want to risk having another prisoner tell him to shut up, an act of disrespect he'd have to respond to.

"In Marion you just really don't have too much

communication," he said. "And sometimes you feel lost and then the people, they not really functioning right. People tend to age a lot at Marion, they worry. They don't wanna be here. People be loving their families and they can't call them. It's lonely here." Rayful couldn't call his family anyhow, because they had been spread far and wide, to prisons as distant as California.

"I'm going through the hardest," Rayful said. "Probably harder than anybody else been through, but I don't let it bother me. I just try to be me, just be Rayful. Like a lot of people come to jail and they get caught up into what's happening in the institution, but that's not what life is about. Life's about being free and living in the streets.

"If I ever went home, I would never come back. I'm just here until one day when I catch a break, get back in court and maybe get some of the time back and have a date to go home. I just be thinking of that. I'll get out in a couple of years from now, probably two years." But Ray was dreaming.

"Everybody is trying to make it seem like drugs is all that bad. I'm saying it is bad, when it gets to the kids that don't know what it is. It's bad. But when you of age, it's not bad. When you of a certain age, it's not bad. When you of age you make your own judgment." Rayful said.

"People abuse anything in life. Like men have good women and they abuse them. People have nice kids and they abuse their kids. So that's just part of life and a way of life. People be trying to survive, then you got a lot of money, so somebody might try to rob you and kill you. Drugs are all over now. That's just life. They are everywhere.

"I would say white people are more conservative and tend to handle it a little better than black people. Maybe their system be a little stronger as far as with drugs. I don't try to judge people. People just look for ways to survive. And if drug dealers do wrong, their intention is not to hurt anybody, not to hurt kids.

"People just say, 'Drugs are bad.' But it's so many people that are out there talking about, 'Drugs is bad,' that are using drugs themselves. Just like Marion Barry. All this stuff he going around talking about drugs this, drugs that. I've been locked up for years and the streets are worse than ever. If I was the problem everything should have been cleared up by now."

In 1990, after a short stint at U.S.P. Marion, Rayful was transferred to U.S.P. Lewisburg where he had more freedoms like walking the yard, using the phone and having the run of the compound. Not much, but better than 24 hour lockdown. U.S.P. Marion was the maximum security prison in the federal system while U.S.P. Lewisburg was only a high security institution. Rayful settled in nicely to the less restrictive environment.

"He came in with great accolades," an old time mobster who was at the prison when Rayful came in says. Lewisburg is a very gothic style prison, like an old English castle. Hawks and other birds of prey inhabit the steeples built into the structure. Also there is a historical wall that can't be altered. The wall is 50 feet high. The population at Lewisburg when Rayful arrived consisted of Italians, Asians, blacks and Irish. All the major ethnic groups were represented and Lewisburg was a hub of criminal activity as it is located between all the major East Coast cities and the most densely populated areas.

"All illicit activities are going on there because all the major cities are a stone's throw away," the old time mobster says. "The prison housed some of the most famous prisoners of the United States from Jimmy Hoffa to John Gotti to biker leaders from the Outlaws, Pagans and Hell's Angels. Big drug dealers from all the major cities were there including Peanut King, Little Melvin, Big Melvin Stanford, Cadillac, the Nicky Santoro crew, Sam the Plummer's crew, Jimmy "The Gent" Burke, members from all the five families, the big Colombian dealers and a lot of guys from the Raymond Patricia family, Frank Valente, Angelo Leonardo and Joe Gallo. John LaRocca's Pittsburgh family with Nick the Blade and the Philly Nicky Scarfo crew were there. The gangs weren't popular then."

Ray quickly took advantage of the situation. He learned that it was even easier to deal drugs from behind bars to people on the outside. He had access to phones on the B cellblock practically whenever he wanted. There was the mail and there was his full contact visits. All privileges he didn't have at Marion. He got his visitors to smuggle small amounts of cocaine, heroin and marijuana in to him.

"Those were the basic four: cocaine, crack, heroin and marijuana," he said. Rayful brought the drugs in through the visiting room. He hired other prisoners, whose girlfriends, during contact visits, would pass the drugs packed in small balloons. It was a simple routine. The oldest trick in the book.

"She might kiss him, and he put 'em in his mouth. Got 'em all inside. Then he get back inside the institution, he spit 'em up. I've seen somebody bring in like 60 balloons before. It keeps the jail mellow. Keeps people patient. They be able to get high and chill." Rayful said.

Lewisburg was the center of criminal activity on the East Coast. When you have a bunch of people of such a high magnitude from the criminal underworld in one place illicit activities are going to occur. "Drugs were so prevalent people developed bad drug habits to wash away the memory of their sentences," the old time mobster says. "There were crap games, alcohol- homemade or smuggled in, every drug imaginable. They even had a Monte Carlo night, where you could play blackjack or dice like in a casino."

Making the most of his circumstances, Edmond reinvented himself, becoming a broker- bringing inmates with sources of cocaine together with his friends and associates back home who had the customers. "I wanted to make more money," Edmond said. "At that time my mindset was I had to still have people look up to me and prove that I was still capable of making things happen."

Ray wasn't in Lewisburg two weeks before the FBI started getting reports that he was still dealing. The clever Edmond just moved his office to the penitentiary. He was doing the same thing from prison. And he found dealing drugs was even easier from prison.

Just a few short months after arriving at U.S.P. Lewisburg, Rayful met the man who would propel him into a whole new realm of drug dealing. Sharing the cellblock with Rayful was Dixon Dario Trujillo-Blanco. His brother Osvaldo, known as Chicky, was just a cellblock away. The three quickly became friends.

"He had a high profile case. I had a high profile case," Rayful said of his introduction. "This is Chicky. This is Ray." Rayful quickly bonded with the brothers. After all, they had a lot in common. Besides similar convictions for drug dealing, all three were mama's boys, raised by tough women who taught them the drug trade. They were young, powerful, connected and infamous.

The Trujillo-Blanco brothers were sons of Griselda Blanco, an influential figure affiliated with the Medellin drug cartel that was headed by Pablo Escobar. Dubbed the Godmother of Cocaine, Griselda was considered royalty in the drug trade and also one of the most notorious players in the cartel's U.S. operations. She was one of the first big dealers to work on U.S. soil for the ruthlessly violent and progressive Medellin Cartel. Her story has been profiled in the popular *Cocaine Cowboys* documentary.

Like Edmond's mother, Bootsie, Griselda rose from humble beginnings. Bootsie peddled pills on Washington streets, Griselda worked as a pickpocket in New York when she first came to the U.S. in the 1960s. The Trujillo-Blanco brothers were also introduced to the drug business at an early age. Griselda turned to her top financial advisor and her favorite hitman to instruct her sons on the distribution and killing end of her business. With similar upbringings the young drug barons formed a new venture, but the new venture was right up their alley.

Lewisburg was crowded with convicted drug dealers and the dealers were doing a bustling business inside the prison, setting up deals for friends on the inside and outside. The Trujillo-Blanco brothers would become Edmond's new Colombian cocaine connection, a replacement for his suppliers from the Cali Cartel, who went to prison when he did. The game didn't change, only the players.

"It's amazing," an FBI agent said. "Prison is like a college where people with similar backgrounds and interest meet and became friends." When Edmond met the Trujillo-Blanco brothers, the brothers were two years away from being paroled, but they had plenty of drug connections to offer.

"His cellmate was one of the biggest Colombian drug dealers and Rayful was a kingpin from D.C. It was a natural business relationship." Smoke says. "Ray became a big power broker, he would block off hours at a time to talk on the phone. He would talk to 50 people at a time. They treated Ray like a godfather. He kept on dealing even after he went to federal prison for life."

Rayful masterminded the shipment of more than two tons of cocaine from the coca fields of Colombia to the District of Colombia from his cellblock. He took advantage of every privilege at U.S.P. Lewisburg, using the phones to arrange introductions of Washington dealers to Colombian suppliers. He was networking on overdrive.

He often made 60 calls in less than five hours, occasionally using two lines at once. His contacts on the outside set up conference calls for him to Colombia and he used the prison mails and visiting hours to work out details of the meeting of the various parties.

One afternoon Ray made 54 calls to four states and two foreign countries. He spoke Pig Latin to his homeboys in D.C. to circumvent the prison phone system's monitoring system. It was too easy for Rayful.

"People are sitting in prison, making drug deals." Rayful said. Rayful was getting $1,000 commissions on the deals he brokered. "I wasn't making the money that I should be making. But you know, I was getting five grand here, ten grand there, which is good money for somebody that's in jail, and they're doing time." Rayful said.

"He was exceeding that which he did when he was

running what had been the largest drug operation in D.C. history." U.S. Attorney Eric Holder said. "He was doing about 400 kilograms of cocaine per month while in prison." Prison didn't stop Rayful Edmond, it made him bigger.

"He was giving this person 200 keys, this person 100 keys, this person 50 and it would all be gone," Smoke says. "He was bringing 500-1000 kilos of cocaine a month into D.C. Bringing it in raw and uncut."

The feds said Rayful sold over 19,000 pounds of cocaine from his cellblock in federal prison. "It was much easier to sell drugs in prison," Rayful said. "Because you're right there where the people that have direct access to the narcotics that you need- Colombians, Cubans, Mexicans."

By October 1991, a tipster had told federal authorities that Edmond was back in business. From April to October of 1992, the FBI listened in on four prison phones as Edmond brokered deals between the Colombian brothers and various drug traffickers. Federal authorities caught fleeting references to Bootsie and Griselda Blanco amid the arcane codes Edmond and the Trujillo-Blanco brothers used to arrange large cocaine deals.

The Trujillo-Blanco brothers were paroled in early 1992 and went back to Colombia. To reach them Edmond simply made collect calls to Washington area associates who patched him through to the brothers via conference calls. Two of those associates were Michael Jackson and James "Jim-Jim" Corbin, both of whom lived in Suitland but supplied cocaine to the District's Trinidad neighborhood.

"Chicky went home to Colombia," Smoke says. "Because of his connection to Chicky, Ray could have

20, 30, 40 kilos sent to D.C. at a time." Jackson and
Jim-Jim bought almost 500 kilos of coke from Chicky
through Ray in the months of January through October
1992 and wholesaled it to D.C. dealers. Jim-Jim would
travel to New York and Florida to make drug pickups and
Chicky would send couriers to D.C. to collect payment.

In July 1992, law enforcement officials intercepted a
drug payoff between the two, seizing $120,000 in cash.
But busts were the cost of doing business. As long as the
primaries weren't caught, business continued.

For his role as matchmaker, Edmond collected
commissions based on the amount sold. His commission
payments were picked up by various other associates who
distributed the money as Rayful directed, to friends and
family members and to lawyers to whom Edmond still
owed money.

"His name was still ringing in the city," D.C. Chris
says. "After all, he was one of the biggest dudes to come
out of the city. His crews name was still ringing too. Still
does for that matter on a respect tip." As Rayful's name
rang in the streets he did his thing from prison.

"I just enjoyed it," Rayful said. "It was something for
me to do. I was in jail and I had nothing to do. It's just
about everybody inside the jail in some way, shape, form
or fashion is dealing drugs, either directly or indirectly."

Rayful also acted as a mediator between the Colombians
and the Washington dealers. "Dudes weren't paying him.
They were like fuck you. There was several millions of
dollars owed to Chicky for the drugs, but Chicky didn't
blame Ray." Smoke says.

In mid-1992, Rayful persuaded Chicky not to kill
Jackson and Jim-Jim, who had not paid for cocaine
delivered to them. Instead the Colombian upped his

price by 10 G's a kilo- to 26 grand- to make up for his losses. Osvaldo "Chicky" Trujillo-Blanco, 25, was unfortunately gunned down a few months later in a Colombian nightclub to Rayful's detriment.

"Chicky was killed, assassinated over an argument over money. Ray was devastated by the news," Smoke says. "There was a number of problems with the money. With Chicky gone his people wanted the money and Ray was responsible. Ray sent out a message, 'You better pay or you'll be in here with me.'" It was said Ray had a debt of $7 million to the Colombian dealers.

The feds were on to Rayful big time also and were actively building another case against him. On October 21, 1990- less than a month after entering Lewisburg- a telephone monitor who listened to one of Edmond's telephone calls submitted a written report to the SIS office that, "Edmond was talking to Squirrel about what seemed to be drug deals." The SIS report stated that, "Edmond says just because he is locked up doesn't mean he can't get what he needs." The report also noted that Edmond was on the hot list at the time, a list of inmates that deserved special attention from SIS. SIS stands for Special Investigation Services and they act as the investigating arm of the custody staff.

After receiving the report from the officer, the SIS lieutenant at Lewisburg made a note to the file on November 1, 1990 indicating that he needed to consult with the FBI regarding what appeared to be continuing drug activity by Edmond. The SIS lieutenant reported that he consulted with FBI special agent Richard Rodgers, who was assigned at that time to investigate criminal activity at Lewisburg.

Because of Edmond's extensive drug dealing history

the SIS lieutenant spoke to Rodgers about "what to watch for and how to proceed" with monitoring Edmond's activities. The SIS lieutenant said that Rodgers advised him to keep a close watch on Edmond and report any additional suspicious activity to him.

The SIS office picked up "continuing intelligence on Rayful Edmond utilizing phones to continue drug trafficking operations." On October 17, 1990 and January 19, 1991 telephone monitors wrote additional reports about suspicious activity by Edmond.

Edmond was never punished for any of these telephone calls, despite the fact that the Bureau of Prisons noted that many of Edmond's calls from prison were three way calls that were prohibited under Bureau of Prison regulations. Federal authorities were busy focusing on other U.S.P. Lewisburg inmates who were also apparently jamming the prisons phone lines making drug deals.

In August 1991, a former FBI informant incarcerated at Lewisburg contacted the FBI in Washington D.C. to report that Edmond was dealing cocaine from prison. Based on this information, Rodgers and other FBI agents obtained copies of Edmond's previously recorded telephone calls from Lewisburg.

In April 1992, the FBI and the Washington D.C. Metropolitan Police Department began six months of court authorized interceptions of the telephones in Edmond's cellblock. During this time, the FBI learned that Edmond was arranging drug deals from prison through his Colombian friend Chicky.

Explaining how Rayful had been allowed to build another drug empire from prison using monitored phones, FBI agent Rodgers explained, "Rayful Edmond was not perceived by me to be any significant criminal individual in which the FBI may have had an interest, as he had just been sentenced to prison, he was simply one of many drug dealers, even large scale drug dealers, who was confined at U.S.P. Lewisburg."

Rodgers also said that the approximately 1200 inmates housed at Lewisburg placed more than 80,000 calls a month. Given this volume of calls, Rodgers said the FBI would generally not open an investigation based on a single suspicious phone call by an inmate. In general, the feds worried more about the violence in prison, than the drugs. Their main focus was to keep prisoners from killing each other.

When Chicky was assassinated in October 1992 in Colombia, this cut off Edmond's supply of cocaine. Consequently, the FBI suspended its investigation of Edmond and refocused its attention on the remaining co-conspirators. Thereafter the U.S. Attorney's office for both the District of Colombia and the Middle District of Pennsylvania decided that based on the evidence that had been accumulated at the time, it was unlikely that Edmond would be indicted on new charges stemming from his activities in prison.

Since the feds didn't pursue the matter the Bureau of Prison didn't take any action against Edmond or restrict his calling privileges in anyway. So Rayful kept doing him. Even without Chicky and the Colombian connect he was making moves. He just switched from one resource to another. He was in drug dealer central so it wasn't a problem. He was Rayful Edmond after all.

In July 1994, the probe swung back to Edmond's associates Michael Jackson and James "Jim-Jim" Corbin. Edmond's girlfriend and five others were arrested after Edmond was allegedly duped into setting them up with an undercover police officer. At the time a defense attorney for one of the six defendants in that case insisted that Edmond had turned government snitch.

"I knew," James Rudasil said. "But his persona is so strong. Rayful is the ultimate stand up guy. That persona just sucks people in. Rayful Edmond would be the last person anyone would thank was a snitch." Law enforcement officials insisted that Edmond had been duped and the streets could never believe Rayful was a snitch anyway. He was D.C.'s pride and joy, their charming and charismatic gentleman gangster.

In April 1994, the feds had sent an informant to get close to Rayful. The FBI began using the informant in an undercover operation targeting Edmond and other U.S.P. Lewisburg big willies, Nelson Garcia and Cali Cartel leader Freddie Aguilera, who were running a cocaine importation ring from the pen. Finally the feds decided to do something about the kingpins dealing from prison.

After extensive investigation and the seizure of a multi-kilogram cocaine shipment near Newark International Airport, the FBI and the U.S. Attorney's Office investigating the case requested that Bureau of Prisons officials remove Edmond, Garcia and Aguilera from the Lewisburg population in order to conduct searches of their prison cells. They wanted to put them on ice to build their cases against them.

"The feds sent a nigga named Donald 'Worthy' Wortham to set up Ray in Lewisburg," D.C. Chris says. "After the Colombian dude Chicky got killed, it slowed things down in the city for a second. Through Ray, the city was getting blessed by Chicky. The feds knew this but couldn't get to Ray, until Donald caught a case and couldn't do the time. They knew that Donald knew Ray so they sent him to Lewisburg and Worthy hit him with the good story. 'I got a man that has the money, but his connect is not steady.' Ray bit and plugged Worthy's man (the feds) in with the connect."

While held in segregation, the FBI confronted Edmond with the evidence of his drug trafficking in prison. "The feds went to Ray and let him know he was through," D.C. Chris says. "Told him he was going back to Marion and that his appeal on the first charge didn't mean shit. That's right the whole crew was coming back on appeal except for a few people."

When authorities ensnared him in the July 1994 sting, Edmond saw that as a chance to break his addiction-selling cocaine. He never used the stuff, let alone smoked a cigarette or drank a beer and with his man Chicky being gunned down in a Medellin nightclub, Rayful must have been tired of it all, the hassle, the hustle, the deals- living up to the name Rayful Edmond and being the big wheeler dealer everyone expected him to be.

Edmond offered to cooperate with law enforcement officials. "I don't condone snitching," the D.C. hustler says. "But if a man is in prison and he is providing you with assistance and he only wants 1,000 dollars, pay the man, they putting him under the gun." Rayful was between a rock and a hard place and took, what he thought was his only escape path.

"I had been giving it a thought for a while that I wanted to stop selling drugs and I figured this was the best way for me to stop," Rayful said. Rayful, a D.C. street legend and icon, did the unthinkable. He started working for the feds. In the penitentiaries and in the streets dudes couldn't believe it.

Part 9

Working for the Feds

"They took Rayful out of the prison and had him brought to a hotel. We discussed with Rayful the evidence we had against him," an FBI agent said. It was truth or dare time for Rayful. He had to put up or shut up and take it on the chin.

"Ray told them that he was thinking about it for a long time," Smoke says. "He told them, 'I'm gonna say what I need to say to get my mother home.'" But D.C. Chris disagrees. "All that shit about he did it for his mom is propaganda by the government. The muthafucka snitched," he says.

Sources familiar with the investigation said that Edmond agreed in principle to switch sides in 1994. The deal became official in early-1995 and Edmond began reaching out to Washington area dealers, mainly those who had turned up on the government's 1992 wiretaps. Except this time he was working for the feds.

The FBI applied to the Department of Justice for approval to use Edmond in undercover operations at Lewisburg. Nelson Garcia and Edmond were subsequently returned to the population at Lewisburg. Before being returned to population, Edmond had to sign a release in November 1994 stating that he believed himself to be safe on the compound. From the compound, with his full phone privileges, Edmond cooperated with investigations of drug trafficking in and out of prison.

"I was fucked up with I heard Ray had flipped." Yo said. "I actually found out he was fucked up, because during the time he flipped I had just finished up a five year lockdown control unit program at the ADX in Florence, Colorado. They ended up sending me to U.S.P. Lewisburg. Rayful was still there when I arrived. "The SIS kept me in the hole and wouldn't let me out for shit. I was like damn I got enough of this lockdown shit at the ADX; I'm trying to hit the pound. The officer didn't say shit he just looked the other way. Finally after three days of this bullshit I got my answer.

"The officers came and snatched Ray off the pound during count time. I saw the U.S. Marshal's from the courts take him away and I'm like ain't this some shit. The next day the SIS called me out of my cell and said, 'Yeah, Yo, Ray works for us now.' All I could think about was slim let these muthafuckas rape him.

"I told the SIS, okay, what the fuck you telling me for, all I'm concerned with is when the fuck I'm getting off lockdown. The lieutenant in charge said that I was never getting out of his hole. Then this muthafucka told me that Ray told him not to let me out, because I might see that something wasn't right with him and they wasn't gonna jeopardize their investigation. They ended up shipping me to U.S.P. Atlanta, Georgia."

Edmond's cooperation resulted in numerous arrests

and convictions of drug traffickers, including the indictment of six people in Williamsport, Pennsylvania and the arrest of ten others in Washington D.C. Two of the drug traffickers arrested with Edmond's help were Freddy Aguilera and Nelson Garcia. "That's why I say when your life is on the line I realize now that you got to do what you got to do." Rayful said. "I'm going to look out for myself a little more, especially when I ain't done nothing wrong." Rayful was fully committed to Uncle Sam. He flipped the script and changed sides mid-story.

Edmond told his friends that he was back in business with Dixon Trujillo-Blanco. Many of them knew that Edmond had lost his connection to the Medellin Cartel when Chicky was killed, but they didn't question Edmond when he told them he had reestablished ties with the surviving brother. To dudes in D.C. a Colombian connect was as good as gold and they were trying to fulfill their street dreams by any means.

"Niggas was happy as shit," D.C. Chris says. "Ray called and said that Chicky's brother was in town. Shit, niggas was glad as a muthafucka. All the time a nigga think he's meeting Chicky's brother, he's talking numbers with the feds. Them bastards tricked everyone. Kept a nigga on hold for months, they would call once and a while and tell you be ready. All that good shit."

Five men- Marcus Haynes, Lecount Jackson, Adolph Jackson, Darrell Coles and Rodney Murphy took the bait Edmond offered, and each went to Lewisburg to meet with him. All but Murphy had met the Trujillo-Blanco brothers before, having bought hundreds of kilograms of cocaine from them, with Edmond acting as a broker. To them it was just Ray hooking back up with the connect.

"We gained tremendous intelligence when Rayful Edmond said to the FBI he wished to cooperate with the government," Assistant U.S. Attorney John Dominguez said. Plus the feds got all his resources and street info. Ray could tie up a lot of loose ends for the authorities. The immediate results of Edmond's work were the arrests in D.C. of 11 people, five of whom authorities described as the biggest drug dealers in town. Edmond set them up and arranged for them to meet an undercover agent, D.C. Police Detective Jesus Gonzalez, who posed as a representative of the Trujillo-Blanco family from Colombia.

The men and their associates met with Gonzalez in Newark to work out the details of their purchase of 60 kilos of coke for $1 million with $375,000 to be paid upon delivery. With Rayful's assurances and their confidence in who they were doing business with, there wasn't any room for doubts. They dove in head first. The drug dealers came to the delivery site on August 8, 1996 with nearly $200,000 in cash as down payment on the 60 kilos of coke. They were promptly arrested and the money seized. As FBI agents questioned one of their associates, his beeper kept going off, flashing codes apparently sent by customers anxious for delivery. Authorities noted that the five apparently trusted Edmond completely, none were carrying a gun when arrested. Although many of them were teenagers when Edmond was in his heyday, a law enforcement official said, most of them knew or had dealings with him.

"I consider myself a loser," D.C. Chris says. "Not only did I see the police that day. I just didn't want to believe it. And of course being greedy and loyal to the niggas I was with. But I'm a loser because I don't have a pot to piss in or a window to through it out of. I've learned that if you heard a nigga was hot and he went and put work in and smashed the dude for saying it, it doesn't mean he ain't no rat. It just means he's a tough rat." Christopher Johnson aka D.C. Chris ended up getting 150 months for being caught in the sting operation and the knowledge that he was set up by the biggest drug dealer from the city ever, Rayful Edmond. The others arrested that day were Jimmy Robinson, Anthony Smithers, Derrick Hopkins, Richmond Deane and Johnny Cherry. All victims of Rayful's betrayal of the drug game.

"Any drug dealer then and now would enjoy doing business with Edmond. It would be a claim to fame," DEA agent John Cornille said. "I could see how each and every one of them would like having that on their resume." Cornille said he wasn't surprised that Edmond was able to get back in business so quickly and that he could still tap into the district's cocaine trade seven years after leaving for a federal prison cell. That Edmond would cooperate for his mother was in character, Cornille said. When Edmond was arrested in 1989, "He was interested in pleading guilty in exchange for a cap put on the sentences of his mom and his three sisters. But the offer was not accepted." Cornille said. "He would know how hard prison had been for his mother. That could wear on a man." Especially one who was as devoted to his mother as Edmond was. Until he went to prison, Edmond had never lived more than a couple of miles from her. "I always wanted to see her free." Rayful said. And he did what he had to do to make that happen.

Notorious D.C. Drug Dealer Turns Informer to Aid

Mom; Edmond Sets up 5 to Cut Her Prison Time, The Washington Post headline read. *The Washington Times* trumpeted a similar headline, *Jailed Kingin's Deal Frees his Mother: Edmond Helped Authorities Break International Drug Ring.*

The possibility that Edmond was cooperating with authorities had surfaced previously two years before, but no one had believed it. Edmond agreed to help the government if federal authorities would use his cooperation as a reason to ask a judge to reduce his mother's sentence. U.S. Attorney Holder said that authorities agreed to the deal, but that her status was up to the judge who sentenced her. In truth though the feds always say that. It was understood by Rayful, set people up and your mother goes free.

His mom, his sisters, brothers, brothers-in-law and others, were all in the family business with Edmond, and were serving time. This was something Ray always regretted. He felt good in making the effort to try and free his mother. His mother and sisters were together at the Alderson Prison Camp in West Virginia.

The feds told Edmond they would not recommend a sentence reduction for him, but they agreed to go to bat for his 56-year-old mother. "That's my mom," Rayful said. "You know I love her and I miss her. I wanted to put it all behind me. I wanted to help my family. That was the first thing that gave me my motivation- my mom, my aunt and my three sisters."

Edmond's devotion to his mother was legendary. He kept sending money to her even after they both went to prison. "I feel honored," Bootsie said of her son cooperating to get her out. "I mean, he has life and he didn't think about himself. He thought about his mother." No surprise for those who knew Rayful. They knew he was a dedicated mama's boy.

As the 11 D.C. dudes Edmond set up were being arrested, he was pleading guilty to conspiracy charges. On August 8, 1996 Edmond and another dealer from Atlanta were convicted for conducting drug business from a federal prison phone. Edmond received an additional 30 year sentence. He testified that both Lecount Jackson and Marcus Haynes approached him to link them with the Colombians so they no longer had to purchase cocaine from dealers in D.C.

Michael Jackson and James "Jim-Jim" Corbin were also indicted with four others in an indictment in Pennsylvania for their dealings with Rayful. In cooperating, Edmond kept doing what he had been doing from his cell at the maximum security Lewisburg prison. Assistant U.S. Attorney Steven J. Roman said he believed Edmond finally regretted what he had done to his hometown by selling cocaine and helping others to sell it. "He has quite a bit of remorse at this time." Roman said. Rayful had fully and unequivocally joined Uncle Sam's team.

"It is intolerable that criminals who were incarcerated for the precise purpose of protecting our citizens have instead been able to use the prison facilities as their home offices for creating and commanding narcotics enterprises that have left nothing in their wake but death and destruction on the streets of our city," U.S. Attorney Eric Holder said, upon revelations of Edmond's activities.

For Jailed Kingpin, A Cocaine Kinship, The Washington Post headline read. "Today's events demonstrate the shocking fact that inmates in a federal correctional institution have been able to participate in international conspiracies from behind prison walls." Holder said. He also announced that Rayful had agreed to forfeit $200,000 of the profits he had racked up during his prison cell dealing. As a reward for his cooperation his mothers 14 year sentence was reduced. There was no discussion of cutting Rayful's sentence.

"Edmond was such a notorious figure it was unpalatable for the government to consider reducing his sentence." Assistant U.S. Attorney John Dominguez said. They did do him one favor, the feds put him in a little known witness protection program for convicts.

"I was in Lewisburg with Rayful and when I got out the nigga was calling me trying to get me to do some things with him on the coke tip. But I had just got out and wasn't trying to hear that shit. I'm glad I didn't cause that was when he started setting niggas up," Smoke says. "He was setting dudes up and getting good men a lot of time. They said that the Colombian Chicky got killed for fucking with Rayful. His people knew that Rayful was a snitch. The Colombians put a hit on Ray."

But Rayful was living under an alias in a different prison where it was hoped that those he betrayed wouldn't find him. "I could stay in here 100 years and it's not going to change anything," Rayful said. He was bitter at his life sentence, but felt a lot of satisfaction at being able to help get his mother out. Even if it ruined his legacy forever.

Convicted Drug Kingpin Now a Government Witness, Edmond Tells all, The Washington Post headline read. Edmond was testifying at a federal trial of three defendants, a woman accused of being a courier and two men who were incarcerated at U.S.P. Lewisburg with Edmond. As part of his cooperation agreement he had to tell the feds everything he knew.

The men- Nelson Garcia, a Cuban in his late sixties and Freddie Aguilera, a Colombian in his fifties- were already serving long sentences when they hooked up with Edmond and tried to sell cocaine through his contacts on the outside. Garcia, who was serving a life sentence, and Aguilera, who was serving 60 years, sought out Edmond because they heard that he had eager buyers whom they could supply with cocaine.

On cross-examination, attorneys for the two men attempted to rattle Edmond and even anger him. One of the attorneys, Phillip Masorti, got a rise and a rather nasty look out of the government's new star witness, when he insinuated that Edmond might not be able to read. For the most part, Edmond rolled with it and gave as good as he got. He got back at Masorti by asking whether the defense attorney knew the meaning of the words that Edmond used.

At first Rayful appeared nervous. He kept leaning forward into the microphone to answer questions, even though it was already close enough to him, making his voice boomerang around the large courtroom. Initially he kept his answers short- showing that he was a well coached witness. But he became more animated and started to appear more relaxed, lounging in the witness box and studying his nails as defense attorneys asked him questions.

He even interrupted his answers to say, "Bless you" to a female juror who sneezed. He reverted to the Rayful Edmond of old, the charmer even though his once basketball players trim body was more bulky, his face fuller. Still he was as meticulous as ever about his appearance. Sporting dreads and a trimmed beard. He had come full circle.

Edmond's case represented one of the most notorious abuses of phone privileges in prison and was an embarrassment for the Bureau of Prisons. Edmond told the feds that during his six year stay at Lewisburg, the institution only had collect calling and inmates could call anyone who would accept the charges.

He said telephones were available between the hours of 6:30 a.m. and 11:00 p.m. daily. While most inmates did not have access to telephones during their work assignments, Rayful said that some inmates- himself included- worked as orderlies within the housing unit and had access to telephones throughout the day. With his status and his homeboys backing him, Ray had the phone on lock, exclusively for his own personal use.

Edmond said that during his incarceration at Lewisburg he talked on the telephone "all day long" and made arrangements for drug deals almost everyday, including participating in conference calls to Colombia. Edmond claimed that he arranged to have drugs brought into Lewisburg 50 or 60 times. He estimated that almost half of Lewisburg's inmates were involved in bringing drugs into the institution, claiming that inmates used each others friends to deliver the drugs.

"The temptation is there, you got people everyday, different people coming here to hook up drug deals." Rayful said. "I wanted to help my family." And Rayful did that by sending his mother and other relatives' money he made by brokering the deals. He said that most of these drug deals were arranged by telephone. According to Edmond, more than half of inmates telephone use was for "doing wrong," not for staying in contact with their families.

Edmond said that he had little concern about conducting drug deals on prison telephones because he knew that most calls were not being monitored. He believed that his recorded calls would only be listened to if prison officials had other intelligence that gave them a reason to listen to the calls. Edmond also said he was not concerned because he knew that the telephones were monitored for internal security of the prison and not to prevent inmates from dealing drugs on the outside.

At worst, he thought, he would lose his telephone privileges for a short period of time or be put in the special housing unit if he were caught violating the Bureau of Prisons' telephone rules. He said the prospect of these light punishments did nothing to deter him or other inmates from using prison telephones to arrange drug transactions.

Edmond said that even if his conversations were monitored, the guards would not know that he was conducting drug deals because they had no "street knowledge." He said that rookie guards and the guards working in prisons located in rural areas, who had no contact with the urban environment, were particularly unfamiliar with the language used in such telephone conversations.

He said that within a two hour telephone conversation, the details of a drug deal may be expressed in ten seconds, "You should see my new girlfriend. She is six feet tall. She lives down where we used to live on 22nd Street," was the example Rayful used. This seemingly innocuous statement meant that he had six kilos of cocaine to sell for $22,000 each.

According to Edmond it typically took 10 to 15 telephone calls over two days to arrange a drug delivery into the institution. Bits of necessary information were passed through multiple calls to make arrangements, confirm details and check on the people involved. Edmond said that some of the telephones at Lewisburg were also monitored by video cameras, but that inmates learned which cameras were broken because fights and stabbings that occurred in view of the cameras did not result in any disciplinary action.

Similarly he said, monitoring cameras in the visiting room were easily avoided because the inmates knew where the blind spots were and visitors and inmates passed drugs in those parts of the room. Edmond said inmates also used the mails to pass money and drugs in and out of the institution, often taped inside the binding of magazines.

Due to the feds investigation into Edmond's phone use and his cooperation with them, the Bureau of Prisons enacted new phone policies in 1999, including allowing each prisoner only 300 minutes a month. The new phone regulations and restrictions, including the 300 minutes a month limit, were the direct result of Edmond's snitching. So everybody in the Bureau of Prisons today can thank Washington D.C.'s finest, Rayful Edmond, for that.

Part 10

Legacy

"Rayful's gonna have to spend the rest of his life in the witness protection program." Smoke says. "When it got out that Rayful was snitching all the love turned to hate, dudes started saying slim was a faggot and all types of shit." The world class baller and notorious drug dealer was now a super snitch. A disgrace to his city and homeboys.

The Edmond lore of fancy cars, gorgeous women and basketball stars was no more. His rise and fall became synonymous with the crack era, the epidemic it spawned and the ultimate betrayal of the hustlers' street code. Rayful broke D.C. residents' hearts when he broke the no snitching code.

"I hope they are all proud of themselves," Yo said about snitches. "They no longer can look in that mirror of life and stare deep down into their souls without seeing complete chaos. There's no more death before dishonor for you tough guys, because you let the SIS, SIA and the U.S. Attorney's Office rape you of your manhood. And yes, this most definitely goes out to my ex-partner, Rayful Edmond, as well. A rat is a rat."

Rayful was the undisputed king of district drug dealers during the 1980s and his name still elicits controversy whenever it is mentioned. The old image of Rayful swaggering through D.C. streets in fancy threads and expensive jewelry, with a beautiful woman on his arm, was destroyed. Rayful became Ratful. He was a witness for the prosecution. A rat, a snitch, a Valachi.

"Rayful's legacy to me is a bitch," says the D.C. gangster. "He put a black eye on the face of D.C. His antics single handedly gave out-of-state bammas the green light, and weak bitches the green light to get down first. What type of shit is that? They even got fake gangsters on TV, making bitch-ass movies portraying bitch-ass dudes talking about telling, snitching and ratting on dudes in D.C. Why not, huh? One of our own set it off."

Edmond means different things to different people, even to this very day. But he is most definitely an urban D.C. legend whose true life story is far from imaginary hood myth. To some he was a provider and genuine person who could make friends with anybody. A man of morals in his own right, who cared deeply for his family and possessed an undying love for his mother. He was very giving to the youth of D.C. A person that was very unselfish with money.

But Rayful was also a person that was feared because of the power he wielded due to his position. Rayful was king of the city, the drug tycoon and mob boss that a lot of rappers nowadays portray themselves to be. Edmond's sophisticated enterprise moved thousands of kilos of coke and received significant regional and national publicity, making Edmond one of the most infamous drug dealers of our times.

"The city ain't been the same since then. Especially

with that bitch-ass Rayful telling. It almost seems as if he made it a fad. I definitely blame him for that," the D.C. gangster says. "He's infamous for being one of those with the ability and know how, but not the heart to hold true to the code. History in D.C. will always know Rayful for being a bitch, snitch-ass nigga. A sellout and a fraud. We don't remember nothing that he did before the day he snitched. True D.C. niggas don't honor no rats." But some D.C. street legends still have love for Rayful.

"I know Ray don't talk bad about me and I respect that," Wayne Perry said. "I don't talk bad about him, but I can't respect what he did. But still, I don't allow nobody to talk about him around me because I know how suckers work. They be testing the water. Everybody know he is my cousin, so they'll say something indirectly rubbing that in my face. And I ain't going for it, or nothing. So don't think I'm saying something bad about him cause I'm not." And despite his detractors, Ray still receives love from the home team.

"I know that what Ray did, Wayne really don't agree with, but he still loves him and he still respects him, because he knows there's nobody else here that could do it like Ray," Twala, Wayne Perry's girl said. "Ray was a good dude. Ray held D.C. down. Ray was the one supplying and everybody knew Ray held D.C. down. Ray and Wayne was good. When Ray went in, Wayne, he took over as far as dudes that owed Ray money, Wayne made sure that Ray got paid. So they never really had a bad relationship and that's how I really got in contact with Wayne, was through Ray.

"Because we spoke to him like everyday. And even now that they don't see each other or talk to each other, through letters they still show love. Wayne doesn't speak bad of Ray at all because that's still his blood and not only that, but he respects Ray. He just don't agree with what he did." And if Wayne Perry, a gangster's gangster, has love for Rayful, it's not surprising that other people still defend his actions.

"Ray wasn't into the murder thing. Ray didn't order no murders. Ray was a good dude," Twala said. "Ray never really got down with the murder game. If he could eliminate problems he would try to, but some things was out of his control. But he still wasn't down with that. I know he didn't order nobody to be killed, he had too much money, what the fuck, why would he kill somebody and he had enough money.

"And Ray wasn't the type of dude that a muthafucka wanted to kill, because Ray was a good dude to everyone, Ray was a loyal dude as far as being on the streets. Ray was a humble dude and an honest dude. He never fucked over people." But still Rayful Edmond's legacy in the drug game as a snitch will be everlasting, no matter the lip gloss applied.

"It's really fucked up for me because I care about Ray," Twala said. "Ray is a good friend of mine. In my eyes I don't look at him as a snitch. I know I don't really fuck with snitches, but it's niggas in the streets that I've probably talked to and don't know and some I do know, so as far as them pointing the finger, and believe it or not if Ray came home tomorrow these same niggas would be in his face. They would be riding his dick.

"Ray didn't take muthafuckas down like a lot of people did. I think that clarifies the difference in my opinion of a snitch. What he did, I think he did it for his mother and it's a lot of muthafuckas that do it for nobody, they just do it just cause."

That's Twala offering her opinion, but she brought up a good point. Maybe not a good one from the convict point of view, but in Rayful's case accountability was lacking across the board. Not making any excuses for Rayful Edmond, but why would people run off with work from a man already serving life and put him in a bad situation?

Dudes in the street will say, "Charge it to the game," but they are talking about a man's reputation. Did they really expect him to take the loss lying down and possibly lose his life violently as a result of their actions?

Being a man of honor requires much more than simply not snitching, but in the drug game there is basically only one rule, and that rule is don't snitch. So anyone who violates this rule is vilified. Tony Lewis offers some clarification.

"I recognize that a lot of young dudes that are in the game don't have any good examples of morals and principles to help shape you. A lot of the older dudes out there who had any respect or credibility have broke weak and sold their souls to the devil." There was no mention of Rayful, but his ex-partner's point was clear. And Rayful's crew is still held in high regard by the streets.

"None of us can pick the hand we would like to hold. In life, the cards are dealt and you must simply play the game," Yo said. "And play we did. For years I have longed for money, revenge and a sense of acceptance. Not from my crew or from my family, but from society as a whole. Growing up in the streets provided me the opportunity to see life through jaded eyes. Eyes that would one day become corrupt. As I remember what was, I can recall my passion for money and my passion for revenge. If I must be honest, I am proud to have been a part of something that most people only imagine or experience when they watch a movie."

To a lot of people, Rayful was noble in his own way. To sacrifice his reputation, his livelihood, everything he built to that point for his mom, was on the surface, extraordinary. But was that the root of it all? That was what the feds would have you believe. On June 2, 1998, Constance "Bootsie" Perry, Rayful's mom was released three years early because of her son's cooperation.

"I'm sorry and I'm very remorseful for what I did," Perry said before U.S. District Judge John Garrett Penn ordered her release. "I see drugs and fast money should not be a part of my life. I should have known better."

Bootsie was wearing a blue prison jumpsuit and dabbing her eyes with a tissue while addressing the court. "My whole life changed in prison." She told the judge and several of her friends and family members said, "Thank you," when the judge ordered her release.

"I hope you take advantage of this," Judge Penn said. "I will," Perry said. None of the eight people in the courtroom associated with Perry wanted to comment on her release. Law enforcement sources said Perry should be concerned for her safety.

"She'll need to be looking over her shoulder for the rest of her life," a source said. Bootsie, who served nine years of her 14 year sentence, slipped out the east door of the federal courthouse in Washington wearing a long blond wig to elude the media and for her own security.

Judge Penn granted her early release based on a motion by Assistant U.S. Attorney John Dominguez. Edmond negotiated the deal in which his mother was granted leniency instead of himself. Mr. Dominguez noted that an agreement to reduce the sentence of a third party was rare, although it had been down before. "We do this only rarely. There have been a handful in the country." He said. In addition to Edmond's help and testimony during three trials in the District and Pennsylvania, Edmond also helped the Federal Bureau of Prisons in its investigation of lax security in federal prisons. He was an equal opportunity rat.

"I hope that if he had been a hero to those youngsters, that he be less than a hero at this point," Judge Penn said. But the legacy of Rayful lived on. *No more Big Willie, my game has grown/prefer you call me William/Illin' for revenues Rayful Edmond like/Channel 7 News, round seven Jews/Head dead in the mic, forgetting all I ever knew*, Jay-Z rapped on *Can I Live from Reasonable Doubt*, keeping Ray's name alive in hip-hop.

In 2002, Rayful emerged from the federal witness program again, this time to testify against Rodney Moore. Moore was charged with being a part of the violent Murder Inc. crew that ruled D.C.'s streets through ruthless killings in the late-90s. Rayful testified that Moore was his one time friend and protégé.

The courtroom was jam packed with people, who just wanted to get a glimpse of Edmond as he testified. Edmond told jurors that Moore, "would offer to kill. I never took it seriously and would tease him about it." Edmond further testified that things changed in the late-1980s when Moore stabbed a man at a bowling alley because he was late paying Rayful for drugs.

Edmond told how Moore visited him in prison. "He was looking to buy 50 to 200 kilos," Rayful said while testifying for three hours in the government's attempts to show that Moore and his partner Kevin Gray were involved in a drug operation despite their lack of physical evidence. It was alleged that Rayful testified in the case to regain visiting privileges with his mother. *'80s D.C. Drug Kingpin Testifies in Murder Trial; Rayful Edmond Alleges Defendant was Protégé, The Washington Post* headline read.

Despite his transgressions, Rayful was still a mythic figure in D.C. and in the annals of gangster lore. His infamy and notoriety were well covered and publicized. Edmond was to Washington D.C. what John Gotti was to New York, an almost iconic figure, whose fearless, flashy style fascinated even those who condemned him and the way he amassed his fortune.

"There are a lot of people that remember the Rayful Edmond story," Smoke says. But unlike similar stories, Edmond's was one that had been little told. No book was written and no film ever made. Yet his life and the spectacular trial that changed it were like nothing the city had ever seen and D.C. native Kirk Fraser set out to chronicle Rayful's legacy in *The Life of Rayful Edmond*, which was released in 2005.

"This is the first real movie about D.C." Fraser, a former Howard University student said. "It's about Edmonds rise and fall in the game. How he made it and what brought him down." Instrumental in the making of the film was Curtis "Curtbone" Chambers, a defendant from the original case. The film received positive reviews, even though it was said to be sympathetic to Rayful.

In the film both Ray's attorney and Curtbone describe how Ray didn't really understand how much evidence was piling up against him. Ray thought because he didn't actually touch the drugs he was safe. Fraser felt it was his duty to touch base on a story that was so much a part of D.C. history. With so much grey area to explore, Fraser felt it necessary to explain why Edmond means different things to different people even to this very day.

"The way I look at the situation is like the past is the past. However, I know some folks will always be curious and fascinated about our story and the shit we did and allegedly done. I guess I can understand why some people still talk about the case. It was an interesting ride. That's why I decided to write my book. If there's an honest dollar to be made. I'm all for it. I'll rather see good men like us get some legitimate paper instead of those cheese eating muthafuckas. They're some damn good soldiers out there with a story. It seems like more people are willing to talk about a rat rather than a good stand up dude." Yo said.

Edmond was not an angel, nor was he a devil. Most importantly, he was not a fictitious character from a movie. He was a real person who may be a different adjective to different people- snitch, drug lord, street legend- the myth of Rayful Edmond encompassed all these terms. If anything he is an icon.

Edmond has emerged as one of the most recognized persons in the last 50 years of Washington D.C. history and his life and legacy has truly impacted the streets as we know them. The legend has endured among the many who lived through those times, and good or bad, few people have had the impact on the city that Rayful Edmond did.

"He's a historic icon," Smoke says. "I grew up around him, when he was coming up. He was that dude for real." Still others look at Rayful in less flattering terms, the image of who he was and what he did leaves a bad taste in their mouth.

"History will remember Rayful Edmond as a

turncoat, a coward, a snitch." The D.C. gangster says. "He is the reason Rome is so hip to us, the true players and macks in the game. As one of those who broke down like a bitch and gave Rome the upper hand.

"Remember how Rayful Edmond and those like him got a lot of warriors fucked up. I know I will. He snitched because he was fucked up that dudes in the streets owed him money and wouldn't pay. He didn't do that shit for his mom. We don't recognize hot bammas. A rat is a rat anyway you look at it and slim is a world class snitch."

About the past, legends and hip-hop in general, Edmond's partner Tony Lewis sums it all up. "I do feel that most rappers are trying to pay homage to the fallen men whose names they use in their songs. But I would like to see the rappers include more of the full story so the young people can see there is no winning in this vicious game. Like how most of us are serving life sentences and have been locked up for decades now. Our choices have affected our children and families. No amount of money, cars, bling or fame is worth your life being taken away." He said.

Rayful Edmond was the mastermind of the largest organized drug ring in D.C. history. As a teenager he did business with Colombian drug suppliers, ironically destroying the same Northeast neighborhoods he grew up in, while at the same time helping the residents, by paying rent and buying clothes and food for them. He was a contradiction in term, a Robin Hood for the hood.

Almost everyone on his case is home now. "Everyone besides Tony Lewis and I are home now. They were released before the crack law was implemented." Yo said. "Jerry was released a few years ago. It's just Tony and I. We're definitely still fighting in court. Hopefully they will give us some act right. We deserve it." Of course Rayful is still in also, hiding out in the BOP's witness protection program or cheese factories as they are called. But Rayful's legacy lives on.

Open air drug bazaars and grotesque killings that plagued the city's spiraling drug trade, couriers going to L.A. by plane to buy kilos of coke, carrying suitcases stuffed with so much cash they could barely carry them and seizures by law enforcement totaling nearly $4 million in cash were the lore of Rayful's reign. He has a legion of devoted fans even to this day.

"Those kids will still tell you I'm a great guy." Rayful said. "A lot of kids from my community, they look up to me and think I was right for selling drugs. I want them to know I was wrong." So if there is a moral to this story, that is it. Because Rayful is definitely reaping what he sowed. Still the legend persists. The Rayful Edmond crew's exploits were legendary in the city where stories about their drug dealing and penchant for violence led to them having street star status.

"It's a good feeling to know that after all these years I can still look in the mirror and love the reflection I see... a lot of so called good dudes no longer share that sentiment. The Jones blood runs through my veins with the same morals I had the day I came to the pen...death before dishonor." Yo said. But in the end Rayful couldn't live up to the image that he created. He was a big wheel of the drug trade and a role model, but he crumbled under the weight and expectations of being Rayful Edmond, by turning into a government snitch.

"It's like this with me," one of the dudes Rayful set up, D.C. Chris says. "If you're in the game period, not just drugs, but anything illegal. When your ass gets caught, shut the fuck up and stand the fuck up. Go to trial or cop out but don't drag nobody else in on your part. You crab ass nigga. That's for all the hot niggas reading this." And Rayful's own man, Yo, his enforcer and head of security sums it all up, "The only thing I would like to say is if you can't do the time, please stay the fuck out of this game."

Sources

- As Quiet As Kept by Antonio "Yo" Jones
- Dream City: Race, Power and the Decline of Washington, D.C. by Harry S. Taffe and Tom Sherwood
- The Life of Rayful Edmond, May 3rd Films
- gorillaconvict.com blog
- Ray- The Rayful Edmond Story, Street Stars
- The Washington Post
- BET's American Gangster series
- Court Records
- The Washington Times
- 60 Minutes
- The Washington Post Magazine
- As Is Magazine
- Don Diva Magazine
- wikipedia.org
- Streetz Magazine
- Department of Justice Report
- Zimbio.com
- Bouncemag.com
- Panachereport.com
- Bet.com
- F.E.D.S. Magazine

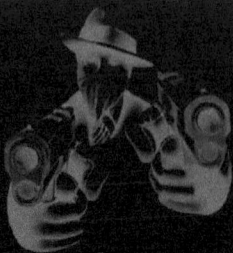

Diary of a Motor City Hit Man:
The Chester Wheeler Campbell Story

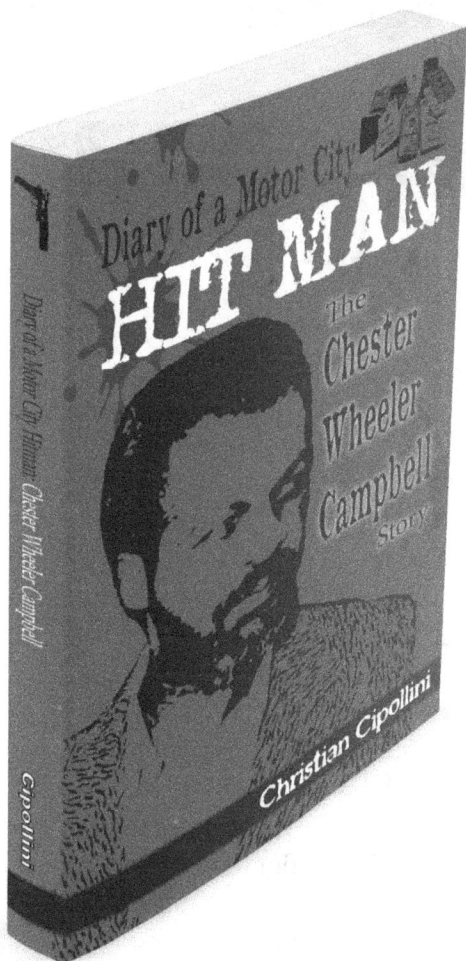

DEALER
COURIER
SPY
MASTER
OF
DISGUISE
LADIES MAN...

HIT MAN

by
Christian Cipollini

www.diaryofamotorcityhitman.com

Excepts from

Street Legends Vol2

Chapter 1

Frank "Black Caesar" Matthews

In the 1970s the heroin market in the United States was dominated by one man, a black distributor named Frank Matthews who operated out of New York. He was the most notable figure on the east coast at the time and one of the first major independents who challenged the Mob for supremacy in the criminal underworld. The Black Caesar, as he was known, was a new kind of super-criminal ruling a nationwide empire of dope. He was the boss of bosses and the DEA ranks him as one of the Top Ten drug traffickers in United States history. A pivotal figure in the history of the drug trade, Matthews was one of the nation's largest narcotics dealers from the 1960s through the early 1970s, and he routinely handled multi-million dollar shipments. More importantly, Matthews was the first black man astute and confident enough to control an interstate organization the size and scope of his operation, at a time when the Mob controlled everything, illegal or otherwise. Astonishingly Matthews did it while still in his twenties. He became a major dealer in twenty-one states with quality overseas contacts for both heroin and cocaine. Frank was a North Carolina country boy who seized control of the black rackets in New York City. The DEA said that Matthews imported heroin from Turkey by way of processing plants in Marseilles, France and cocaine from Latin America. Street legend has it that his wealth could not be counted. He had Pablo Escobar-type money in the early 1970s. It didn't go to his head. To him money wasn't but a thing. He controlled the illegal drug market in the inner-cities from the east coast to the west coast and had contacts with Cuban wholesalers who controlled vast portions of the South American coke trade to the United States. Matthews earned respect in the streets and criminal underworld by holding his own against the Mafia. When his profits became so huge that they took notice he didn't bow down, he dictated. In essence, Frank was the first black man that had the Mob shook. He was a true trendsetter and set the standard for future street legends who followed in his path and tried to earn the title of American gangster.

Part 1- Country Boy

Frank Larry Matthews was born on February 13, 1944 in Durham, North Carolina, a poor segregated town in the heart of tobacco country. His mother died in 1948 when he was only four-years-old and his aunt, Marcella Steel took him in and raised him as one of her own. The section of Durham Frank was from was called Mohead City. He lived down the street from Mohead Baptist Church and attended East End Elementary School. His whole family hailed from Durham and they called the youngster, Pee Wee.

His aunt, who was married to a cop on the Durham City Police Force, treated Frank like a son. He grew up a bright and curious kid in a family of five with his uncle the cop and two cousins. The boy called Pee Wee as a youth because of his scrawniness, would grow to full size physically and become a giant mentally. By junior high he decided that school wasn't his thing and dropped out after only a year. He knew his path would lead him elsewhere, even at that young age.

Frank was inspired by a rock-and-roll singer named Clyde McFadden who grew up in the same area and left Durham for New York City. Clyde returned twice to his old neighborhood after he made good to show off his fancy clothes, his shiny new Cadillac and his big roll of bills. Clyde made a big impression on Frank, if Clyde could do it then he could too Frank decided. In the seventh grade, before he dropped out, Frank was already dreaming big. He wrote an essay that outlined his plans to become rich and settle in South America. His future was set but first he had to make his name locally.

Little Pee Wee was a born leader, who was capable of organization and had mesmeric powers of leadership. He recruited all the neighborhood kids including his cousins and got into all kinds of mischief. Frank was the type to inspire faith and loyalty, all the young boys rallied around him and he became a shot caller at a young age. His crew plotted on the Farmer's Market, which was across the street from the ball park. Frank and his homeboys wanted to rob it. At 14, Frank's first act as a shot caller was to organize a gang of eight and nine-year-old homeboys to raid local chicken coups. Eventually a white farmer found out Pee Wee was leading the raids and tried to teach young Frank a lesson, but Frank wasn't having it. With gangster in his blood even at that young age he threw a brick at the farmer and busted the older man's head wide open. This incident led to Frank's arrest in October, 1960 for stealing chickens and assaulting the owner of the chickens he stole. Even as a kid Frank Matthews was not to be trifled with. He served some time at the Raleigh State Reformatory for Boys on that offense and upon his release he bounced. The country boy was moving to the city at the age of 17, but he kept in touch with all his homeboys, who he'd later recruit for his drug ring.

Part 2- Move to the City

Frank went to Philadelphia first. In Philly he got a job as a numbers writer. He quickly learned that with a piece of a policy bank he could clear $100,000 a year. His homeboy Thomas "Cadillac Tommy" Farrington followed him to Philly. The lifelong friends embarked on a journey into the criminal underworld watching each others backs on the dangerous streets in the City of Brotherly Love. While there Frank established what would be his major Philly contacts who were all associated with the Philly Black Mafia- John "Pops" Darby, Tyrone "Fat Ty" Palmer and Major Coxson. Frank was networking and making connections but he got busted in 1963 on a number of charges and had to leave town. Due to the influence his new contacts had with law enforcement the charges didn't stick, but Frank still had to bounce. His next destination was New York City, otherwise known as the Big Apple. Frank settled in the Bedford-Stuyvesant area of Brooklyn and worked as a barber, running a numbers ring out of the barber shop. He worked as a barber in Philly too and knew it was a good cover/ fall back option. Plus he could generate contacts, meet new people and learn who was who. This led to him taking the next step in his criminal career. He started working as a collector-enforcer out of the barber shop on Tompkins Avenue. The kid they called Pee Wee had grown into a man and became so handy with his fists that other fringe characters in the Brooklyn underworld recognized and acknowledged his gangster by getting him to collect debts owed, with a percentage going to Frank of course. The kid from North Carolina was evolving into a tough, lean gangster with no fear and no objections to busting heads when and if he had to. It was all about getting what he wanted and what Frank wanted was money and power.

"Frank came up from North Carolina. He was in the numbers game." A dude we'll call Fats, who was around in that era says. "He was an enforcer-type guy back in 1965. He hung around up on Tompkins.

Frank could be a mean motherfucker when he wanted. Dudes were kind of scared by him. They didn't know how to take him, but he could be real cool also. He muscled his way into the racket and started backing the ticket." At 5-foot-9 and 180 lbs, Frank was like Mike Tyson in his prime. He quickly put his gorilla down in Bedford and people took notice. "They called him the Book in the streets," Fats says. The Italian Mob controlled most of the numbers action in Bedford-Stuyvesant and that was who the recently migrated country boy found himself working for. "He did numbers for us," an Italian mobster from the era says. "A tough kid. He was a charismatic dude. Got his people to do things his way, which was really our way. He was smart, organized. We used him to settle the blacks down. He controlled them in Brooklyn like Bumpy did in Harlem." The Mob thought they had a pawn but Matthews was much more than that. He was the hustler who would be king.

By 1966 Frank was well established, so established that he was arrested by the police. But the charges didn't stick. Frank learned that money made most problems go away. At 22, Frank knew that all problems would melt in the solvent of money. With this knowledge he become Teflon coated in the borough. He made the necessary moves to stake out a piece of Brooklyn for himself, as well as use it as a base for what he had in mind. Frank Matthews didn't think small, he dreamed big, Technicolor dreams in an age of black and white. He was a man of action and in the back of his mind was an idea for an out-of-town network, that would supply dope to ghettos across the nation.

"You could always tell that Frank was scheming." Fats says. "He wasn't no surface-type nigga. He was a deep guy." Frank already had the contacts in Philly. When he went to New York, his homie Cadillac Tommy became closely aligned with several Black Mafia heavyweights and became Frank's top man in Philly. With his widening criminal horizon Frank decided it was time to get into the dope game. But he knew that in 1967 nobody could get very far in the dope game without the Mob behind them. Frank approached some mobsters in New York City for some raw heroin and finances. In the time of Mafia dominance that's how it was done.

"Frank was a very respected guy in Brooklyn." An old head from Bedford-Stuyvesant says. "He treated an individual good. He was a tough guy but he never did no crazy shit. He was a fair dude. I ain't ever met no one like him." The Mob didn't know how to take this young go-getter either. They liked to keep blacks in line and under their thumb and had succeeded in doing just that for a long time. But Frank Matthews would change all that. He was the chosen one long before LeBron James. He would become the Michael Jordan of the dope game. A Machiavellian schemer that wasn't afraid to make a G-call.

Part 3- A Career Change

Young Frank managed to get an audience with the Mob. Louis Cirillo, a Mob heroin distributor recognized Frank's promise and introduced him to the

business. He introduced Frank to members of the
Bonnano and Gambino crime families. "Frank knew
a bunch of them mobsters," Fats says. "At first it
was like he worked under them but that didn't last
very long." The mobsters listened to Frank's plea to
get into the drug game but turned him down. That
didn't stop him. In 1967 he said fuck the Mob and
attempted to set himself up. Since Cirillo and the
Mob turned him down, Frank sought other connections.

As the Mafia's grip on African-American neighborhoods in New York loosened, narcotics distribution in Brooklyn's minority areas was being taken
over by the people who lived there. They were no
longer content to remain in the pay of Cosa Nos-
tra importers and wholesalers. Many were new
customers, looking to their former employers not
just for supplies but for working capital and management expertise as well. Black drug dealers were
organizing, much like the Italians had done in the
1920s and 1930s, with the purpose of carving out a
territory, establishing a clientele and eliminating the
competition. Frank Matthews was a new breed of
criminal, an urban demi-god who was attracted to
the glamour of the gangster life.

"He was from Carolina," the old head says. "He got
a lot of his homeboys and a lot of good guys out of
Brooklyn. I first heard about him because he bor-
rowed a bunch of money from the Italians to get on.
He paid them back so fast that it fucked them up."
The Mob wouldn't supply Frank with heroin, but
they would loan him money at exorbitant interest

rates. By examining the Brooklyn drug markets, Frank took inventory of what was required to gain control of some territory that could function as a supply base for an out-of-town network. Since the Mob wouldn't supply him he bought drugs whenever and wherever he could.